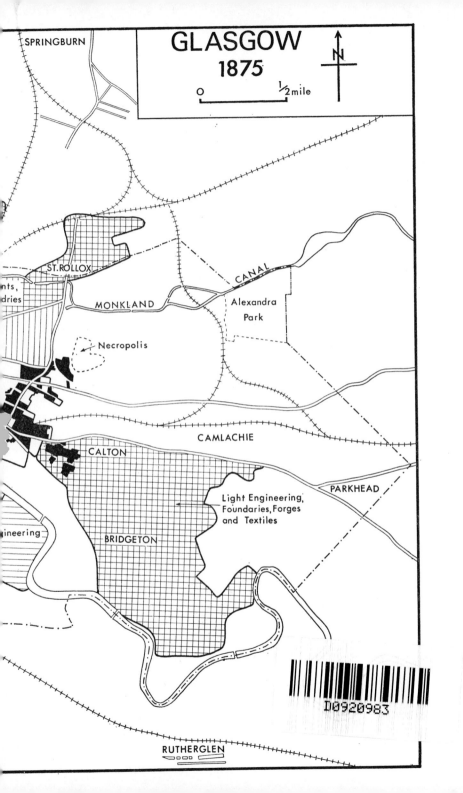

GLASGOW
1875

O   ½mile

N

SPRINGBURN

ST.ROLLOX

nts, dries

MONKLAND

CANAL

Alexandra Park

Necropolis

CAMLACHIE

CALTON

PARKHEAD

Light Engineering, Foundaries, Forges and Textiles

ineering

BRIDGETON

RUTHERGLEN

UNIVERSITY
OF GLASGOW
PRESS

The Upas Tree

For the Staves
   - this small exercise
   in urbanism and
   communalism!

   - from

Olive + Sydney Checkland

January 1977

THE *S. G. Checkland*
UPAS TREE

GLASGOW   1875 — 1975

A study in growth and contraction

With eight illustrations by Muirhead Bone

UNIVERSITY OF GLASGOW PRESS

1976

ISBN 0 85261 133 1

The upas tree of Java (Antiaris Toxicaria), entering European legend through Erasmus Darwin, was believed to have the power to destroy other growths for a radius of fifteen miles. Here it is taken as a symbol of the heavy industries that so long dominated the economy and society of Glasgow.

Printed by Robert MacLehose and Co. Ltd, Anniesland, Glasgow
for
University of Glasgow Press

For
John and Lesley
Ruth, David and Claire

Contents

Illustrations   By Muirhead Bone

Muirhead Bone and Glasgow

MUIRHEAD Bone was born in Partick in 1876, and during the 1890s was apprenticed to a Glasgow architect. He soon gave up architecture to become an artist, but not before receiving that basic training in the elements of construction and the appreciation of detail that was to become such an important and integral part of his future work.

Bone settled in London in the winter of 1901–2, but made frequent visits back to Scotland for the rest of his life; he died in 1953. From 1898 to 1901, when he was in his mid-twenties, Glasgow was the main inspiration of a series of etchings and drypoints which have placed Bone amongst the most famous printmakers of any era. Like the greatest of them he was self-taught. He is known to have looked carefully at the work of Meryon and Whistler, whom he particularly admired. The influence of Whistler shows in several of his early works and particularly in those of the lower Clyde. Bone was concerned with the accurate recording of reality; he drew what he saw. The slums and shipyards of Glasgow had the vitality and overwhelming detail which appealed to him, so that his work has become a true record of a vanished Glasgow.

Bone's drawings were not produced as social comment; he was recording scenes which intrigued him and placed a demand upon his professional skills, so that the content of his subjects seems to have taken a somewhat secondary rôle. In the shipyard prints it is not the concept of work in its sociological meaning which appeals to him, but the excitement of the yards and the complicated structures encased in their scaffolding.

The range of his subjects and the masterly use of the techniques of etching and drypoint have rarely, if ever, been used to capture so successfully the life of a great city. Between *Mike, the Dynamiter* and the Glasgow Exhibition series of 1901 there is an incredible gulf. But each scene is viewed with the same professional detachment and recorded with the same superb dexterity that appeals equally to a general public and to social historians.

Roger Billcliffe

Preface

THIS outline considers the city of Glasgow in its regional context at the great climax of its growth and confidence in later Victorian and Edwardian times, and, with a linking chapter, again in the years between the ending of the Second World War and 1975. Its object is to indicate, in broad terms, the principal elements of Glasgow's experience over the past century, though some reflections on the future appear in the final chapter.

The study has its origin in two lectures delivered in the University of Glasgow as part of the celebrations of 'Glasgow 800', marking the end of eight centuries of Glasgow as a chartered burgh, and its replacement, under the reorganisation of Scottish local government, by the Glasgow City District.

Within the last hundred years Glasgow has presented in sequence two dramatic historical syndromes. There is first that of 1875–1914, a period of cumulative and self-reinforcing growth in which an amazing congruence of circumstances produced the greatest of Britain's provincial cities, a regional metropolis, the second city of the British Empire, and, on the European scale, a ranking in terms of population and productivity within the first six. This has been followed in the years since 1945 and especially since 1960 by a virtual antithesis: a situation in which so many circumstances, instead of reinforcing one another in a positive way, have contributed cumulatively and in conjunction to one of the greatest problems of urban regeneration in the west of Europe.

It was not all success in the first phase to be considered, nor failure in the second. High prosperity before 1914 did not purge dereliction and slums, but left a painful residuum. Nor must the difficulties of contraction be allowed to diminish the more recent achievements of the city, nor obscure the continued vitality and colour of Glasgow life, nor detract from the sustained efforts of so many men and women who have sought to make their varied contributions to the city.

The ever-growing number who want to know more about the factors and processes which govern the fate of modern industrial cities may wish to have Glasgow in their gallery of case studies. For those involved in the challenge of urban renewal, either as students or policy makers, the city provides a marvellous opportunity for clinical observation. For those concerned with the social and political processes that go on as great cities pass through expansion and contraction, Glasgow provides the most striking case in Britain and perhaps in Europe. Finally, the people of Glasgow and the Strathclyde Region may find helpful this attempt to understand something of their own background.

For those wishing to consider further the Glasgow story in these terms over the past century a list of writings is added. It will be seen that the city in recent years has generated a considerable literature within and about itself. But there are serious gaps. A high proportion of the monographs and reports are devoted to physical planning, housing, amenity and welfare; there are fewer studies available dealing with the industrial and commercial base on which all else rests. The political control of the city is another serious omission. There are important monographs yet to be written; a number of attractive possibilities are hinted at.

I have gained much from colleagues at Glasgow University, including R. W. Brash, Gordon Cameron, Kay Carmichael, Olive Checkland, Robert Cowper, Sean Damer, Richard Dell, Tom Hart, Roy Hay, Orla Henry, Robert Holton, John A. Mack, John McCaffrey, Michael Moss, Stanley Nisbet, Nancy Porter, Anthony Slaven, Martin Staniland, Andrew Thomson, Joy Tivy and Douglas Weir. Others who have helped are J. Adams, Isabel Burnside, Hamish Fraser, John Hume, P. M. Jackson, Peter L. Payne, Ian Robert and Louis Rosenburg. William Taylor has made invaluable comments.

The index has been compiled by Wing-Commander R. F. Pemberton. Jean Forbes and Michael Shand have provided the map of Glasgow, 1975. Roger Billcliffe assisted in the choice of Muirhead Bone drawings and has written the descriptive note. It is perhaps appropriate to pay tribute to Bone in 1976, his centenary year.

SGC

Adam Smith Building
The University of Glasgow

I. The Pattern of Prosperity, 1875–1914

1. The city of St. Mungo

GLASGOW is of course an ancient city with its own saint; it received its first charter in the twelfth century; its university was founded in 1451. It lived a modest ecclesiastical life for generations, though producing more than one notable bishop; it shared the travails of the Scottish Reformation. It took a worthy part in the European Enlightenment in the later eighteenth century, especially in the persons of Adam Ferguson, Adam Smith, John Millar, William Hunter, James Watt and Joseph Black, and at the same time provided one of the focal points of the first industrial revolution. It was one of the great cities of Britain throughout Victoria's reign, one of the places where the universals of industrial urban society were first exemplified, but within the distinctive context of Scottish life.

St. Mungo had been the patron of the city over a long and varied experience when, from the 1870s, it entered upon the period of its greatest prosperity and expansion.

2. The conditions of industrial prosperity

Output, incomes and jobs are the fundamental elements of the life of a city and its region. If these are growing in a society in which the state stands largely outside the economic system, there will follow a characteristic set of relationships. There will be a feeling of general well-being and confidence such that success induces further success. Businessmen will be willing to experiment, to initiate, and to invest, standards of living will rise, civic initiative will flourish, local taxation will have little inhibiting effect (for spending on welfare from public funds will be on a minor scale and the tax base on which it rests will be ample), labour relations will be

B

good, contributing both to output and to mutual confidence. Ideological discussion will be minimal, for there will be little incentive to make radical criticisms or to seek a generalised alternative; polarisation between businessmen and workers will not develop to any great extent; unwillingness to produce more lest this add to profits or subtract from employment will be largely absent. But the housing supply for those with low or unstable incomes will be bad. The provision of houses will be a matter of private investment, without tax-based subsidy, and rents will be the outcome of market forces. Civic politics will operate on non-party lines, so that participation is on an individual basis. But it will also be on a class basis, an affair of business and professional men.

By and large, this was the condition of Glasgow in the years 1875–1914, especially down to about 1900. The city was prosperous and proud. Certainly there were blights on this picture. Some of them derived from the experience of the industrial revolution and its aftermath. Some were the outcome of high prosperity itself, together with its consequence of congestion and increasing social casualties. But, all in all, Glasgow in the generation or so after 1875 presented a picture of impressive well-being and confidence.

On what did this growth syndrome rest? In a sense it was an accident. The various elements of which it was composed were not present by any inherent necessity or any coordinated policy. Glasgow then, as now, stood at the north-west extremity of Europe, remote from the great markets of France, Germany and the Mediterranean, enjoying no automatic accrual of wealth as an entrepôt and as a money market, far removed from the great European centres of scientific speculation and application. The people of Glasgow, and indeed of Scotland, had to find the means within themselves of overcoming distance and isolation, to establish conditions of wealth-generation that rested upon their own immediate circumstances.

There can be little doubt that the history of Scottish culture, especially since the Reformation, played an important part. The standard of Scottish literacy, based upon the parish schools, and the stern discipline and self-application inculcated by a Calvinist reformed church, both contributed to a sense of confidence and justification, as well as providing the incentives for application and persistence. These factors were perhaps at their peak in the generation after 1875, giving assurance and incentive to the middle classes of Glasgow, and providing the basis of respectability among many families of the working classes. Counter-ideologies were the concern of tiny minorities until the later years of the century, and even then were scarcely a challenge to the prevailing ethos. The fact of continued prosperity would, of course, have a feed-back effect upon ideology and work performance, making for an alleviation of conflicts.

The element of discipline was real, exercised in a variety of ways. At the factory or shipyard gates the hiring of unskilled men was done in the light of previous performance and sometimes of favouritism; in times of decennial cyclical recession, especially, there was strong and sometimes bitter competition for jobs. Secondly, there was the tradition of the foreman, often a figure around whom legends accumulated, a man who inspired awe in the apprentices and whom the journeymen had to propitiate. In these ways the productivity of the labour force was kept up. A shipbuilder, for example, with a contract to fulfil, could drive his men in the good weather in a way that is today almost inconceivable.

But such sanctions were often not necessary. Much of Glasgow's engineering industry called for craftsmen whose pride and personality were built around their skills and their products, who found a fulfilment in their tasks. A launching on Clydeside was often almost a family affair, the workmen looking on with satisfaction as the ship they had helped to create took to the water. There were, in addition, programmes of paternalism and welfare that bound employers and their workforces together. These applied perhaps especially to foremen and skilled workers who might be provided with housing, and who might well be kept on in bad times so that an all-important cadre of men was kept together, perhaps doing maintenance and improvement until new orders came. Such arrangements would now be described as techniques of social control.

The creation and dissemination of engineering ability on Clydeside was a local achievement. It was not a question of skills and labour being transferred from London or anywhere else, but was a Clydeside creation, arising out of the values, energies and education of the men concerned. It is appropriate to think in terms of great names, men who sought in their working lives to express and promote their private ethic, as with David Napier, the first to combine engineering and shipbuilding in one firm, or Alexander Stephen and his world-encompassing ships. Robert Napier's yard, taken over from his cousin David, was a kind of engineering college, where men like the Elders and Charles Randolph were trained to the highest standards, many going to other firms, spreading their skill and craftsmanship. Many of the shipbuilding firms were on a family basis. But a foreman such as Charles Connell, inspired by his master, could move out and start his own yard; Randolph and John Elder founded Fairfield's shipyard at Govan; likewise William Lithgow, beginning as a shipbuilding apprentice with Russell & Co. at Port Glasgow, was to take that firm over.

Starting, then, from a particular pattern of motivation rooted in Scottish religion and education, heavily imbued with the lowland ethos, and confirmed by the nature of local industry and of local demand, Glasgow produced its distinctive forms of entrepreneurship and of labour outlook. By the 1890s these rested upon a division of function so absolute that it was unthinkable that management should consult labour, much less concede any rôle in decision making. Many great firms were ruled by their founders or by their sons, men who took their authority over their business for granted.

But a regional economy cannot be made to flourish simply on the basis of an ethos regulating the attitudes of managers and men and the organising ability and productive skills this engendered, even when these are as powerful as in the west of Scotland. It was necessary that nature endow the Glasgow region with resources of a kind that could be made economically relevant by developments in technology, capital formation and marketing. Chief of these was the ready accessibility of coal and iron in juxtaposition. This set a strong tradition in the working of ferrous metals, the material basis of engineering.

Finally, appropriate market conditions were required: the Clyde, with its estuary and its access to the Atlantic made possible an initial regional market highly suitable to the steamship, thus providing the basis for subsequent expansion.

Such a convergence of circumstances could produce a pattern of production that could perpetuate itself even after one of the basic resources, namely iron, was approaching economic exhaustion; because coal was still plentiful, and because bulk carriage of ore and scrap was available in the west of Scotland by sea, river and canal, the raw material position, though one of partial dependence, was, at least for a time, secure. Glasgow could continue for a further period as one of the great iron and steel centres of the world because her natural position made this possible in an evolving situation. The output of steel from Motherwell, Cambuslang, Coatbridge,

Gartcosh, Mossend and Wishaw, all within a few miles of Glasgow, rose from 50,000 tons in 1879 to 1,250,000 tons in 1911; steel capacity further doubled between 1911 and 1918. The 'Iron Ring' could continue to be one of the great elements in the Glasgow Exchange, providing Britain with a Prime Minister in the person of Mr. Bonar Law.

The second of Glasgow's great natural advantages was its geographical position, highly appropriate to the other elements of her situation since well before the 1870s. She had been Scotland's window on the Atlantic, a rôle which she developed yet further, trading to North America and indeed the rest of the world. More than twenty steamship lines had sailings to all the world's chief ports and many of the lesser.

The natural advantage of her eastern hinterland, based upon coal and iron, was thus complemented by that of the Clyde, her western gateway. In Glasgow there mingled the traditions of mining and metal working with those of the high seas. It was of course the steam engine that brought them together; the virtuoso production of engines to replace sail, even on the longest routes, created a kind of unity of hinterland and outlet: like Venice, Glasgow had her empires *da mar* and *terra firma*, each part of the other; in Glasgow's case they were wedded by the steam engine.

On this basis there arose a classic example of external economies. An extraordinary level of engineering skill was generated, so that Glasgow could build and power both ships and locomotives of an extremely high level of performance. The relations between local industries were those of mutual assistance, through the provision of mutual services. The focal points of this consummation were marine and locomotive engineering, and the shipbuilding of the Clyde. The former pair represented the most sophisticated development of mechanical engineering, and the latter an immense industry of assemblage without standardisation of parts. With these at the centre of the economy of the city and region, other elements were grouped around them: machinery manufacture for coal cutting, sugar processing and many other uses, all with their ancillary service trades. Of the four greatest locomotive building firms in Britain, three were in Glasgow: in 1903 they united to form North British Locomotive, the Titan of its trade. Civil engineering, especially bridge building, was a Glasgow *forte*, led by the firm of Sir William Arrol: from Glasgow came the Forth and Tay Bridges, the Tower Bridge, and many of those on the uncompleted Cape-to-Cairo Railway. There were celebrated foundries, achieving virtuoso feats in iron as at the famous Saracen works. Behind all these lay the great iron and steel enterprises and the producers of semi-finished goods: plates, bars and tubes. The mighty Parkhead forge was the core of William Beardmore and Co., which took over Robert Napier and Sons in 1900 and began naval construction at Dalmuir a few years later.

It was shipbuilding that caught the imagination of the world, giving Glasgow a special image summed up in the expression 'Clydebuilt'. Before 1870 the annual tonnage completed on the Clyde had been less than 200,000; by 1913 the figure was 757,000 tons with indicated horse-power of 1,111,000. Some 40 firms, great and small, crowded the banks of the Clyde. Their capacity exceeded that of all the German yards taken together, both in tonnage and in engine power; the Clyde was responsible for one-third of British tonnage and one-half of its engine power. The young Muirhead Bone sketched the yards and fitting-out basins with their fantastic masses of frames and hulls, the timber scaffolding, the spindly sheer-legs, the smoking chimneys and the vast engine shops, all stark and grey against what a contemporary called 'the engineering skies of Glasgow'.

These were the yards that performed the feat, so incredible in retrospect, of developing a vast complex of shipping construction, of world fame, much of it miles up a minor watercourse artificially created. It was done by the unco-ordinated action of individuals and enterprises. They used the principle of adding on, biting new pieces of land from the ground adjoining, generating and employing external economies. They intensified particular skills, creating a strict division of functions recognised by employers and men alike, providing the basis of job demarcation and union organisation.

Together, managers and men put together complicated, highly finished, expensive ships. There were passenger liners aiming at exceedingly high standards of comfort for the first class travellers, and minimum ones for the steerage; the same ship could carry the rich in luxury, glamour and idleness, together with land and work-hungry refugees from Europe in crowded quarters in the stern. There were ships of war embodying the latest and most sophisticated means of delivering and resisting destruction.

Not only were all these made and powered on the Clyde: their engine rooms became the enclosed kingdoms of Clyde-trained men: an echo of this has been apparent on television, in the person of 'Scottie', responsible for the virtually perpetual motion engines of the *Spaceship Enterprise*: the legend of the Clyde ship's engineer has reached final apotheosis in the fantasy world of space travel.

But though in the metallurgical-engineering sectors diversity and adaptation were attaining ever new levels, the regional economy was, almost imperceptibly, losing other elements that had been of great importance only a short time before. Macquorn Rankine had in the 1850s described with great satisfaction the extraordinary breadth of Glasgow's industry, including the two great elements of textiles and the manufacture of chemicals: Glasgow had been, in effect, a Liverpool and a Manchester together – a port, with a coal and iron hinterland, but also with textiles (especially cotton), and heavy chemicals arising originally from the needs of textiles.

But by the early 1870s the decline of spinning and weaving was well begun: the mills that had stood around Glasgow Green, throwing out their smoke and expelling the middle classes to the western suburbs, were by the last decades of the century losing out to rivals at home and abroad. Glasgow's cotton industry was greatly diminished, partly because of its dependence upon female labour, who, as the Factory Inspector observed in 1883, 'cannot stand the strain and fatigue involved in attending to a pair of modern self-acting spinning frames'. The celebrated St. Rollox chemical works had lost its European predominance in output, management and invention and was, indeed, falling behind. Though Tennant's stalk could still tower over Glasgow, the Leblanc process which it served was yielding place to its Solvay rival; St. Rollox was becoming a backwater. Just as nature and changing technology had given their aid in helping to induce Glasgow's shipbuilding engineering ascendancy, so these same influences were withdrawing the basis upon which earlier successes in textiles and chemicals had so notably flourished. But so prosperous was the city, and so great was its confidence on the basis of its engineering trades, that there was little concern that older elements should fall away, their leadership abandoned to other places.

Nor was there, apparently, any shortage of capital, for the major industries of Glasgow could be, by and large, self-financing, at least for most of the period. Short-term money needs could be met by the highly developed Scottish banking system. Though Scottish capital was certainly going abroad on a great scale in the *Pax Britannica*, it was not at the expense of under-provision on Clydeside. Britain was investing in the continued growth of the world economy, a condition that was now essential, given the degree of dependence on foreign trade which the world's first industrial nation had created for itself. The economy of Glasgow was more dependent than that of any other region of Britain on this condition being met. So far as was foreseen at the time, Glasgow was a great beneficiary of a world in which British capital exports helped to fructify economies overseas, thus increasing the world's supplies of foodstuffs and raw materials.

The continued expansion of Glasgow's classic industries required an ever-growing army of workers, from the highly skilled to those who could only labour. This condition, too, was met both by natural increase within the city, and by immigration. The two largest groups of incomers were, of course, the Highlanders and the Irish, both displaced by the obsolescent nature of their rural economies. Men and women flooded into Glasgow, many of them to occupy, in the first generation at least, overcrowded and unsanitary housing. The figures are impressive: in 1871 the population of Glasgow was just over half a million, at 547,000; by 1891 it was over three-quarters of a million at 782,000; just before 1914, at the climax, the magical figure of one million was reached. Some of this growth was due to the extension of boundaries, but it was nevertheless remarkable, supplying industry with labour and posing for the city an ever-increasing problem of social welfare.

But there was also population loss: in the years 1871–1931 West Central Scotland's natural increase was diminished by emigration by 27 per cent. This was on a rising trend, especially in the years 1901–14, a period of peak migration overseas, especially to the United States and Canada; thus Clydeside could not hold its population even at the peak of its prosperity. But seen in the perspective of Scotland as a whole the picture looks rather different, for the nation lost no less than 46 per cent of its natural increase, with the greatest losses in the Highlands and the Borders. The emigrants went, by and large, to places where the opportunities were greater for them even than on Clydeside, namely the United States and Canada.

Finally, among the conditions for Glasgow's high level of output, incomes and jobs, there was the factor of demand. By the 1870s the city had developed extraordinary expertise in what was to be a high growth industry. The world's need for ships (and the British dominance of merchant shipping), together with the other products of Glasgow, metallurgy and engineering, all grew. The ability to make these things, and to deliver them to buyers all over the world, was complemented by the sustained level of need of users, together with their ability to pay, both of which rest largely on the continuous expansion of world trade, itself to no small degree dependent upon British exports of capital.

3. The unperceived warnings

The great apogee of Glasgow prosperity is neatly marked by the first and second of her international exhibitions, those of 1888 and 1901, both held in Kelvingrove Park. In these thirteen years Glasgow stood at the peak of her confidence and achievement. The first exhibition was impressive but rather tentative, with an architectural theme somewhat oriental, but it was visited by the Queen. That of 1901 was a different matter: it was the largest such venture ever held in Britain, drawing $11\frac{1}{2}$ million attendances, bringing gondolas to the Kelvin. It was dedicated to art, industry and science. It featured its Machinery Hall and its Industrial Hall, both reflecting Glasgow's own achievements. Indeed Glasgow as late as 1911/12 could still revel in its engines, those marvellous capsules of power that had evolved on Clydeside, all the way from John Robertson's tiny unit for Henry Bell's *Comet* to the turbines of the *Niagara* and the banked might of the diesels of the battleship *Jutlandia*. The Centennial Exhibition of Steam Navigation in the same year as the *Comet* centenary (1912) celebrated the scale and versatility of Clydeside's construction, from the new Finnieston Ferry to the *Lusitania* and H.M.S. *Colossus*, displacing 20,000 tons.

But by 1912 there had begun a certain erosion of Glasgow's industrial position, though this was not yet seriously perceptible. As early as the 1880s, during the contraction of the world economy then taking place, many of the great engineering and shipbuilding firms were beginning to turn their attention to armaments. By the later years of the century defence expenditure was rising, especially in the direction of the Navy, where the revolving gun turret and other developments were radically affecting naval architecture. The government had for long relied mainly upon its naval dockyards; from 1901, and especially from 1905 to 1914, it turned increasingly to the private sector to supply fighting ships. Fairfield's, John Brown's and other yards, finding they had unused capacity, were eager to meet the government's needs. At the same time, because armour plate, though requiring very large-scale investment, was highly profitable, and because of the specialisms of the various shipbuilding areas of Britain, arms rings were being formed. With these some Glasgow enterprises, such as Beardmore's, were associated. The placing of naval orders on Clydeside was thus becoming subject to two sets of politics – those relating the industry to the government, and those relating firms to one another in agreements and cartels.

Perhaps most important of all, the warning given to the Clyde shipbuilders, through the state of world demand, that they might not be able to maintain their output of merchant ships, was ignored. Like an active and sanguine man given the premonitory warning of a mild heart attack, Glasgow paid no attention to her new dependence upon naval contracts – a demand that had nothing to do with the continuing real economic needs of the world, but which was, instead, a drug – and an untried and highly unreliable one. There was an eager embracing of naval building, causing the industry and the commitments it represented to be extended yet further. H.M.S. *Colossus* was a triumph of the art and science of shipbuilding, but it was also a sombre symbol of Clydeside's excess capacity and over-commitment to ships.

The evolution of the economy of Glasgow between 1875 and 1914 is a classic example of the limitation of business time horizons. It illustrates also the tendency, where circumstances have permitted, to develop a high level of mutually confirming specialisations, to press the advantages of such a situation, to be blind to warnings of its precariousness, and to seek opiates that will allow it to continue. In this way it was possible to ignore the erosion of the fundamental basis of the Clydeside economy brought about by changes in demand, the rise of foreign rivals, and the refusal of other nations to continue in a state of dependence upon British suppliers.

There had been in the economic world of the previous quarter-century no large-scale experience of the dangers of over-specialisation in skills, capital, equipment and markets. Commercial crises there had certainly been, but their effects had been largely confined to the produce markets; it was these which had played so large a part in bringing down the City of Glasgow Bank in 1878. Brief though the period of high success in engineering had been, it had become a datum in the minds of Glasgow men, around which they had built their lives and outlook. They took immense pride in their mighty ships and the engines that powered them; in so doing they could look down on their great rival, Birmingham – landlocked, with its range of miscellaneous small-scale trades, sharing with Glasgow the manipulation of metal, but providing the world with no such grand products.

There are some signs that perceptive men in the service of city government were more farseeing than was the business community. The City Chamberlain (Treasurer) was by this time worried about whether the levels of growth that had been experienced could be continued. Civic improvements were costly: they posed an ever-increasing need to raise money, with consequent rises in the rate-poundage. To this the Chamberlain saw serious limits; he saw the city as committing itself to a trend that might not be indefinitely self-sustaining. It is of some interest that thinking in terms of the regional economy should come from this quarter rather than from the business community, though this was perhaps natural, for the Chamberlain saw the city as a tax base.

Clydeside was not without firms willing to experiment, so that some degree of diversity might be generated. The Argyll automobile made in Bridgeton was one of the highlights of the Glasgow Exhibition Trials in 1901; it did well at the Brooklands Track in 1913. Beardmore's entered the embryo industries of automobile and aircraft making (they supplied no less than 650 planes in the First World War). In so doing they, like Vickers, with which they were in association, had to some degree heeded the warnings implicit in their commitment to merchant shipbuilding, and were seeking to enter new areas. But within such a vast organisation as Beardmore's, with its 45 acres of ground, there were exemplified the problems of the Clydeside complex itself. With so heavy a commitment in the direction of large-scale engineering, how was it possible to develop the managerial psychology to manufacture at a consumer level a product so different in scale and production demands, and so new technically as the automobile; how were the traditional skills and outlook of the labour force to be brought to bear in so different a context?

The North British Locomotive Company had been formed in 1903 in order to strengthen their overseas competitive position. But their main difficulty lay in the fact that the markets they served had developed specialised needs, so that they could not turn to the building of cheaper, all-purpose engines. The result was that even so sophisticated a product as locomotives could not lead into modern production methods of standardisation of parts and integrated production, and so help to alter the outlook of management and the training of men. By 1900 the American Singer Company was producing some 13,000 sewing machines per week in its Clydebank factory, by far the largest in the world. Appropriately enough, the coat of arms of Clydebank featured a sewing machine alongside a ship. Here was a classic example of highly modern industry, but the basic industries of Glasgow were impervious to the lessons it contained.

In fact it was hopeless, at least in the conditions of the years before 1914, to generate within a heavy producer-goods industrial economy like that of Glasgow radically new sectors of a more flexible and responsive kind. While the heavy industries were still prosperous, say to 1900, there was initiative and spare capital enough to permit of a modest degree of experimentation, in a peripheral but not major way. But as high prosperity faded, the capacity of the region to do new things declined. The upas tree of heavy engineering killed anything that sought to grow beneath its branches.

The whole vast complex of Clydeside industries had been created entirely without governmental intervention – the magnates of Glasgow were conscious of power and success; it did not occur to them that beyond a certain point there might be a need for some kind of supervisory intelligence deriving from government. Indeed, any such suggestion would have been hotly resented. On the government side, given the concept of the rôle of the state then prevailing, it was inconceivable that it should be attempted, or even seriously considered. In the outcome, down to 1914, the business men, especially the heads of the great shipbuilding firms concerned with armaments, had begun experimentation in cartels, and the government had placed its naval contracts. Miracles had been achieved by Glasgow and the Clyde: why should anyone want to interfere with their onward course? 'Let Glasgow Flourish' was a sentiment firmly rooted in engines, ships, metallurgy and general engineering.

4. Business leadership

The business leadership of Glasgow in these halcyon years from 1875 to 1914 would make a study of great interest. This was the age of mandarinism in Scottish business generally. The head of a Scottish bank was a figure of splendid isolation; so too were many industrial giants. Sir Charles Tennant, Bt., of St. Rollox, Tharsis, the Union Bank, etc. received treatment worthy of royalty. The Bairds were a self-confident, not to say arrogant, lot, at least in their business relations. This generation were, in large measure, the sons and grandsons of the Whig-Radicals who had fought through the Reform Act of 1832: they were established men, proud of their industrial and commercial background, whose vitality, even with advanced age, could be sustained by success.

But Glasgow was also a speculative place, as the collapse of the City of Glasgow Bank in 1878 had shown: interest rates were much more sensitive in Glasgow than in Edinburgh: it was from the west that the pressure usually came upon the banks' General Managers' Committee in Edinburgh to raise lending and deposit rates: it was through Glasgow that the Bank of England could most effectively bring pressure to bear upon Scottish rates in times of upswing. Partly this was because of the importance in Glasgow of the produce markets, especially sugar and cotton, and of the very large transactions within the 'iron ring': these contributed a special air of volatility. Then there were the demands of western industry for capital: shipbuilders and iron and steel masters were notorious for their financial needs from time to time: the bankers, though in principle short-term lenders only, could not avoid involvement in such 'fixed' positions.

The whole pace of business was different as between Glasgow and Edinburgh; a banker who had held an important post in Glasgow was glad to sink back in the more spacious and leisurely air of Edinburgh. Yet, in spite of a belated challenge in the 1830s and 1840s, Glasgow was never able to wrest the banking leadership in Scotland away from the old capital: the continuum of the past was too great, embodied in the law, the church, the town bases of the landed men, and the branch system coverage of the Edinburgh-based banks.

But though banking was at its grandest in Edinburgh, Glasgow had its high bourgeoisie with an unquestioning self-assurance. The Royal Exchange and the Glasgow clubs were the two *foci* of this confident and exclusive maledom. This group enjoyed low taxation, a virtually free choice of industrial location, minimal restraints on pollution, and vast areas over which the Factory Acts or other legislation had little control: indeed these were among the conditions that had contributed to Clydeside's success.

There was no one from the government, or from the intellectuals of the universities or elsewhere, to challenge what they were doing. They had no corporate consciousness that would extend their horizons beyond consideration of their own particular firms: the Chamber of Commerce was not a place where the great men of Clydeside could find a perspective outside their firms, except on delimited topics having to do with trade. The same was true of civic government: it tended to be left largely to the lesser bourgeoisie. The result was that the minds of the great decision-takers on Clydeside were enclosed by their own concerns and their own families. Even one such as Sir Charles Tennant, who became an international business man on a major scale, seems never to have given any serious thought to the way in which the national economy and its regional components were evolving in the structural sense. Such men appear in retrospect to have been curiously blind to what they were doing, working and thinking within narrow time horizons.

But it is to be remembered that this is true of most men at most times; the psychology of the Victorian and Edwardian tycoons was the outcome of a generation or more of success, largely based upon self-confirming accident. Their philosophy was that if each man of business sought out economic opportunity and pursued it, then the system as a whole would be sustained. This was a projection of their free trade outlook, an attitude appropriate to Glasgow's dependence upon world commerce. And, indeed, they were highly successful in defeating foreign competition, showing a high level of response to challenge.

Consistent with this philosophy there was a striking burst of Scottish business initiative abroad: William Mackinnon in Africa, Patrick Henderson and the Irrawaddy Flotilla Company, David and John Cargill and the Burmah Oil Company, Sir Charles Tennant with the Tharsis Copper Mines and the Mysore Gold Mines. But this meant that a high proportion of Scotland's most adventurous business-making was done overseas, having little direct bearing on the economy of Glasgow. Such cosmopolitanism was incapable of altering the fundamental industrial pattern of the city.

5. Labour organisation and militancy

No serious general challenge came from the workers to cause ownership and management to reconsider its position and that of the city's economy.

Trade unionism in Scotland was at a modest level, even down to 1914. This was true of Clydeside, as of other parts of the country. Beatrice Webb, visiting Scotland in 1892, found Glasgow working men's leaders without enthusiasm. Just as Scottish Chartism had been mild and moderate, so too in the decades of high prosperity there was no great militancy in Scotland.

In the revival of unionism from the 1850s, Scotland's pattern had been distinctly different from that of England. Instead of strong national unions on the 'New Model' basis, Scotland produced smallish organisations, with a powerful sense of local autonomy, loosely joined together on a federal basis. Clydeside workers were unwilling to be bound by decisions reached elsewhere. This made for weakness, for it precluded any national trade union body.

It was this that made for the early formation and the power of Trades Councils: that of Glasgow started in 1858. Strike movements thus tended to be local, across a number of trades, rather than national in one. Moreover, before the 1880s at least, most unions had only a minimal continuous existence, gaining recruitment at strike times and losing it thereafter, providing a minimum of facilities of the friendly benefit kind. Partly this lack of union continuity related also to an unwillingness to pay union dues.

In more strictly Glasgow terms the conditions present in its two great industries, marine engineering and shipbuilding, were such that it was difficult to build a sustained trade union initiative. In the former case there was a relatively high level of skill and incomes and employment was more or less secure. In shipbuilding many of the men were either foremen or skilled workers. The policy of firms in keeping both of these critical elements in their labour force through bad times meant that such men developed a loyalty to the firm which would make trade unionism inappropriate. The lower levels of skill, and the labourers, would move from yard to yard when laid off, thus failing to build up group solidarity. A fair proportion of them were Irishmen. The capacity for effective organisation at this level would thus be minimal.

This is not to say that labour militancy was absent: the men by 1914 had learned a good deal about how to make claims on their masters: the masters, for their part, were developing their own tactics. There was a Glasgow railway strike in 1890; the engineering lockout of 1897 on the Clyde brought the Clyde Shipbuilders and Engineers Association into open conflict with the unions, thus portending more serious difficulties after 1914; the strike at Singers in 1911 was a major disturbance.

Clydeside employers, on the whole, had little sympathy with unionism: the Bairds, the Neilsons and others resisted their formation and continuance. There appears to have been little rethinking among Glasgow business men about the relations between labour and employers, but this too is a subject worthy of investigation.

The city was thus, by and large, a place where a fairly high degree of industrial harmony prevailed, or where, at least, few serious overt and sustained signs of tension, much less irreducible confrontation, were present. In this sense Glaswegians could congratulate themselves in comparing their situation with that of London, where trade union militancy had not only returned, but embraced for the first time since the 1830s and '40s the unskilled groups.

In general the economy of Glasgow presented a picture of notable achievment of masters and men, resulting in a range of products over which the city had a world supremacy.

---

1. *Shipsmiths, Stobcross* (detail) 1899–1900 Drypoint
The men swinging their hammers at the forge are shaping by hand large metal parts to be built into sophisticated ships.

II. *The Quality of Victorian and Edwardian Life*

1. *Housing the people*

THE other great half of Glasgow life lay in the social base of the city, as reflected in its physical shape and especially in its most important component, namely housing.

In this respect, as with the economy, there appears to have been an interlocking pattern of mutually confirming elements. At the basis of things there was nature. The Clyde Valley is a narrow plain, hemmed in by hills and moors which, though full of beauty when the sunshine seeks them out, can be, for much of the time, black and forbidding, unfriendly to human habitation. Useable land was, therefore, relatively scarce: Glasgow was not able to straggle casually across an open plain as did so many cities of North America; it had to conform to nature's contours.

It may be, however, that human and social attitudes have also played their part in determining the physical shape of the city, operating through a preference for easier sites, the land ownership pattern and the attitudes of land owners. After all, land has been much more readily available for Glasgow than for Greenock or Belfast or Hong Kong.

Within the area defined by physical and human constraints, there developed an extraordinary concentration of people, especially at the core of the city. This had become a problem of such scale by the 1860s that certain dedicated men of the city, led by Lord Provost Blackie, worked for and obtained a special agency, the Glasgow Improvement Commissioners, who undertook a programme of clearance: under the Commissioners much of the High Street and the Old Town, notorious for overcrowding

---

2. *Mike, the Dynamiter* 1900 Drypoint
Mike had served a prison sentence for a dynamiting incident in Glasgow. He is seated by the forge shown in Plate 1.

and decay, was pulled down. The bringing of the railways into the city and the building of the great termini carried further the clearances of central Glasgow.

But in spite of all, the density remained extremely high. There were by 1914 no less than 700,000 people living in three square miles, thus creating the most heavily populated central area in Europe. Glasgow was a city of more than Mediterranean crowding, with a large part of its labour force packed into its heart, with little or no working class suburbia. To a large extent, even with its splendid system of trams, Glasgow was a pedestrian city. One of the consequences of this concentration was to make Glaswegians urbanites of a special kind, unique among the provincial cities of Britain, identifying with their city to a remarkable degree, in the European rather than the English manner. Within it, however, there were strong sub-loyalties, to the many former villages of which Glasgow was composed: Maryhill, Eglinton, Govan, Gorbals and the rest. Indeed the city seemed to be composed of its many 'Crosses'.

Within this intense but internally diversified urbanism there operated a particular family budgetary pattern. A proportion of family income lower than in any other major British city was spent on housing. This was a built-in preference, the roots of which await really satisfactory explanation in terms that would distinguish Glaswegians from the denizens of other British cities. In these years before 1914 there were a good many empty houses of a kind superior to those occupied; Glasgow workers' incomes were not conspicuously inferior to those of other cities; yet there was only a slight move to better accommodation at higher cost. In part this budgetary pattern was due to the fact that in many trades wage levels were highly unstable, so that workers tended to settle for premises the rent of which could be met in the bad times, treating the surplus of good times as a windfall, and seldom aspiring to house ownership. To distinguish Glasgow from other cities on this basis would, of course, require that she had a higher component of trades with fluctuating wage levels than elsewhere. Though there is no comparative study, this seems, indeed, likely.

The typical house form, the four or five storey terraced tenement, was highly favourable to a pattern of minimal spending on rents, for it provided obvious economies in the use of space. Moreover, such flats could represent an excellent solution to housing, concentrating the labour force and thus saving on the journey to work, and often providing a close-knit and mutually supportive community. Some 85 per cent of Glasgow's population were born, raised, laboured and died in their world of tenements.

With the continued growth of Glasgow from 1875 there was great activity in tenement building. This meant that there was a very large addition to the housing stock, concentrated in these years. It could be provided, for both population and incomes could sustain it, though house building activity slowed perceptibly after 1900, reflecting a steady increase in unoccupied houses, from 4,943 in 1902 to 19,715 in 1910. The indications are that for every ten houses built 1901–18, four were demolished, a large net increase.

Moreover, it was necessary to take official action to stop deterioration in the standards of tenements. One of the great problems was the 'privy system' – communal earth toilets for each stairway: the Police (Amendment) Act of 1890, along with other legislation, commenced a more determined programme to raise housing standards. The Consolidating (Housing of the Working Classes) Act of the same year largely governed the situation for 35 years. In this way more stringent minimal conditions affecting many aspects of tenement living were laid down, regulating air space, ventilation and lighting, ceiling heights, enclosed beds, common lobbies, and the building of 'back lands' in the hollow squares formed by the tenements. Builders were thus obliged to make amenity provision above that which they thought appropriate in terms of money returns. Indeed, Thomas Binnie, builder, argued that the standard of amenity enforced by the Police Acts made it unprofitable to cater for the working-class market. The number of single-apartment housing units for which plans were passed by the Dean of Guild Court reached its peak in 1901 at 1,338, but thereafter there was a sharp falling away to very low numbers by 1914.

The means whereby the Glasgow tenements were built, and the relations thus engendered between landlords and tenants are as yet very largely unexplored. Was it middle class savings that provided the capital, or was it small-scale 'bondsmen', like publicans, making loans of a few hundred pounds to speculative builders with a rapid turnover? How was the size and design determined: were the builders responding to the demand of potential occupants, or did they impose a pattern by what they built? Whatever the answer, tenement life was continued and confirmed.

In spite of the housing activity of commercial builders, there remained grave cause for concern in the bad parts of the city, including the foot of Crown, Rose and Thistle Streets in the Gorbals and the congested parts of Townhead, Bridgeton, Tradeston and Anderston. These places, contained within fairly closely defined areas, were dense and festering, having the power of debilitation and death. The Church of Scotland enquired into Glasgow housing in 1891. In that year the London County Council defined overcrowding in terms of 2 or more persons per room: one-third of its people fell below this standard; in Glasgow the proportion over-crowded was two-thirds. Municipal investigations were undertaken in 1903 and 1911. But bad conditions persisted.

The Royal Commission on Housing in Scotland of 1917 described conditions in parts of Scottish cities, especially Glasgow, that were desperate: 'clotted masses of slums . . . farmed-out houses, congested back lands and ancient closes'. An almost unbelievable density had been reached. In 1917 there were more than four persons per room in 10·9 per cent of Glasgow's houses, over three persons in 27·9 per cent, and over two in 55·7 per cent; the figures for corresponding English cities were 0·8 per cent, 1·5 per cent and 9·4 per cent. The tenements which contained these 'houses' contrasted with the three to five room terraced or detached houses more typical of England. The people of Glasgow were packed into their homes to a degree unimaginable even in the larger English cities. When, under such conditions family morale collapsed the results were terrible.

2. *Glasgow as home*

What kind of life did the economic and social realities of Glasgow in the years 1875–1914 produce? What kinds of attitudes or outlook did they engender?

One way of approaching the matter is to use the two antithetical notions of unity and coherence of outlook, *versus* separation accompanied by indifference or hostility, to see what elements of each were present. Some kind of balance sheet may perhaps then be struck, from which might come an assessment of the states of mind or consciousness present in the city.

It is said that Glasgow's basic mode of life, tenement dwelling, created conditions under which there could be a real social mix, with workers, professional and business men living closely together in mutual neighbourliness or at least tolerance, their children attending the same schools, so that they understood and sympathised with one another. The tenement, moreover, by producing densities higher than in English cities, made for a smaller and more compact living area. Though there has been no serious historical study of this aspect of Glasgow, there was, apparently, some justification for this view of tenement life, at least in some areas. To some extent, the tenements could bring together social groups – some of them, especially on the middle ground between working class and middle class areas, could contain social mixes that would surprise non-Glaswegians. This could mean, for example, that the doctor was near at hand, living among those he cared for, instead of having his residence elsewhere.

It would seem that though areas of concentration of Highlanders and Irishmen could be identified, there were no true ghettoes; Glasgow was one city. Glasgow, like other British cities, received an influx of Jews from Poland and Russia between 1880 and 1906, men and women who entered furniture making, tailoring and shoe making and repairing. Many of them settled in the Gorbals. They suffered the hard times of alien immigrants, but in the second and subsequent generations, enriched the life of the city. An examination of Glasgow's immigrant groups would make a study of extraordinary interest.

The Church of Scotland and the United Presbyterian Church could be regarded as to some extent unifying forces within Glasgow society, with all or most of their members aware of the dignity and perhaps formidableness of the minister as he bore witness to the duties of men and women to one another and to God. Though here, too, we are without any real study of the situation, it appears that, to some degree, the influence and power of the ministers came back in the years of Victorian prosperity, so that the ground, so largely lost among the working classes as the great cities were being built, may have been in some measure recovered. The ministers of both churches would inculcate the virtues of self-help, work and thrift, and would thus sponsor families in improving their condition. Lord Kelvin, perhaps the greatest scientist of his age, and so a leading exponent of rational inquiry, opened his lectures in the University of Glasgow with prayer.

The Roman Catholic Church could perform less of this unifying function, for it had little coverage in the upper end of the social and income spectrum. But in a sense it was in the more powerful position, for its members certainly went to church, and accepted a strong obedience. It would, like the Church of Scotland and the United Presbyterian Church remind men of the brevity of their tenure on this earth, holding out the promise of the hereafter as a compensation for lack of material benefit in the present. All three churches told men, of all classes, that they should 'live to die'.

The sense of common identity among Glaswegians was strengthened by shared experience: there was a real sense in which Glasgow was one. Men and women of all classes remembered childhood and youth enlivened by a day 'doon the watter', an evening at the music hall, Sunday afternoons listening to brass bands in the parks, rides on the trams, inspection of the statues in George Square, shopping in Sauchiehall Street. The Glasgow Underground, the only such line in Britain outside of London, opened in 1896; it provided the city with a transport encirclement that, in spite of its somewhat minuscule rolling stock, represented the latest thing in urban travel. The Glasgow regiments, especially perhaps the Highland Light Infantry, were a source of general pride, in their service in India and other parts of the empire, and in the Boer War. The University at Gilmorehill belonged to the city; there the sons of humble parents had listened to Kelvin on the laws of thermo-dynamics he had helped to enunciate, or followed Sir William Macewen round his wards. There was a general pride in the city and its achievements, a sense of satisfaction in progressive civic government, a savouring of its daring and vigour. All of these things entered into the impalpable flavour of the city's life. This was sharpened by a sense of rivalry and antithesis: all Glaswegians felt as one when mention was made of Edinburgh, and contested strongly with Birmingham for the title of second city of the Empire.

But to all this there was another side. By and large, there was increasing geographical segregation on a class basis, running counter to the notion of social unity as engendered by tenement life. From the 1820s or '30s the middle classes had moved from their houses in the Old Town and around Glasgow Green; the tendency steadily continued, predominantly in a westerly direction, one of the great axes being Great Western Road. There were thus two Glasgows, sharply distinct, as the tram conductors knew so well – a run up west was a quite different affair from one down east. Much of the colour and the humour of Glasgow life came from this polarisation. There was middle-class migration also to the south, to Queen's Park, Pollokshields, Cathcart, Shawlands and Giffnock. The upper middle class were already jumping well beyond Glasgow to Helensburgh, Troon, Prestwick, etc., depending upon the railway for their access to the city.

Within the city middle and lower classes interpenetrated only to a minor degree: the Sunday parades on Great Western Road had their separate counterparts in walks in the eastern end of the city leading to Glasgow Green. Pedestrianism, in fact, had divided more or less on a class basis.

There was separation, also, in terms of speech: that of Kelvinside had developed along very different lines from that of the east end. In terms of education, though the University of Glasgow was fundamental to the intellectual life of the city, substantial numbers of the sons of the more wealthy were being sent to Oxford and Cambridge. Moreover, the traditional claim that the Scottish educational system was a classless one did not apply to Glasgow. Such reality as it had was largely confined to rural communities: in Glasgow the 'lad o' pairts', contrary to the Scottish legend, seldom got beyond the 3 Rs, unless by untypical good fortune. In the army, officers and men were often strikingly distinct in stature as in speech.

Worst of all there were the Glasgow slums, notorious as early as the 1840s, and becoming more intense and decayed with the generations, in spite of the labours of the City Improvement Trust. The continual influx of Irish paupers was in itself more than enough to counterbalance all efforts at creating better conditions. Even the Trust had in a sense made things worse: by 1876 it had cleared 25,375 houses, and by 1902 had built only 1,646 new ones. Rents moved constantly upward: an average one-room house in Glasgow in the northern district increased from 1s 6d per week in 1866 to 2s 6d in 1902. Yet Glasgow was one of the few cities in Britain to tackle the problem of redevelopment at all. It should also be remembered that many who came to the crowded tenements of Glasgow from Irish cabins, Hebridean black houses or continental ghettoes found them to be an improvement.

Even worse off than those who occupied slum dwellings were those who had no abode at all – men and women who alternated between the poor house and the gaol; such unfortunates would have occasional periods, when flush, in the 'model lodging houses', or would occupy space, on a nightly basis, in 'farmed out houses' – e.g. houses whose owners packed their rooms with derelict humanity. The problem of social decay at this end of society seemed insoluble; it was all too easy for both middle and working classes to accept it.

Because of the diversity of conditions within the city, Glasgow produced a rich variety of human types. One of these was the 'wee bauchle', a man of little more than five feet in height, often with legs bowed by rickets. He was the underweight, undersized inhabitant of the grimmest slums in Western Europe. But having come through the perils of infant diseases, such a man, with his immunity against germs, his slum-sharpened wit and his skill in literally using his head against larger men in public house fighting, had a high survival capacity. At the other end of the scale was the industrial élite, the turners and fitters, the 'engineers'. These were well fed men with powerful shoulders and impressive hands, proudly earning twice as much as an unskilled man, willing in their youth to serve a testing apprenticeship to place themselves in this position.

Plainly, there were in Glasgow before 1914 circumstances promoting both unity of outlook and its opposite. How did they relate?

It would seem, on the face of it, that though there were indeed tensions, on balance there was surprisingly little overt hostility between the elements of society. Employment and incomes were, on the whole, reasonably well sustained. It may be, too, that shared experience, together, perhaps paradoxically, with geographical separation, helped to make this peaceful co-existence possible, especially when everyone met and mingled in the city's centre – a place where business and living came together. Such a situation could permit and even promote toward the city both pride and sentiment that could be held in common by all its classes, both in respect of daily work and output, and with respect to the shared city. At the same time the physical separation of east and west may have lessened the potential hostility of the workers and the misgivings of their employers. The very compression and density of the central part of Glasgow made for a city life that was colourful and lively. Instead of, as in so many English cities, dying when the day's business was done, it was a place of human contact.

There was one group of Glasgow men and women who sought to bridge the gap between west and east ends: these were the philanthropists, people of the middle classes, with their myriad of projects and organisations for the amelioration of working class and pauper life. The list of their concerns seems endless: orphanages, reformatories, hostels, industrial schools, savings banks, libraries, hospitals, dispensaries, convalescent homes, medical missions, societies for the care of the blind, deaf and dumb and the crippled, Bible societies, temperance societies. There was the Model Lodging Houses Association, the Artisans' Dwellings Association, the Strangers' Friend Society, the Discharged Prisoners' Aid Society, the Magdalene Asylum and so on; there were the Foundry Boys, Quarrier's Homes and the Boys Brigade (founded in Glasgow in 1883).

The philanthropists were, of course, the products of their culture: they were strongly infused with moralism. But there were also those among them who took a realistic environmental view, exploring the conditions of life of the less fortunate, and seeking remedies. They were the driving force behind the various housing inquiries, trying to find some basis for constructive action. In so doing some found their minds moving in the direction of using the state, with its potential for subsidy, because of the impossibility of solving the problem without such financial backing. Some, too, in desperation, advocated the use of state or local authority power, proposing the segregation into special areas, of the most anti-social families, so that the communal damage they did might be minimised. There can be no doubt that there was a problem of social control in the sense that an unprecedentedly great number of people had been gathered in the city, and that within it there was a tendency for deterioration of living conditions and general behaviour to be concentrated in certain areas – the slums.

Two leading views are possible with respect to the housing efforts of the Glasgow philanthropists and of the Town Council. The public health and humanitarian motivation of such activity has been stressed or implied by many historians. The alternative view is that the provision of housing was part of a system of repression, appeasement, exclusion and control – that it was a weapon in the class war by means of which the bourgeoisie could consciously divide the working class, bringing the skilled men (the 'labour aristocracy') round to their view of society and so dividing the proletariat that it became ineffectual in the pursuit of its real interests, that is the conduct of class warfare.

It is certainly true that Dr. James Burn Russell the Medical Officer of

Health (1872–98) and others, felt and expressed a need to try to control
the situation as best they could so that deterioration and unsocial behaviour
might be contained so far as possible. In so doing they took powers of
inspection and enforcement that certainly seem drastic to a later generation.
But Russell and his contemporaries had inherited a problem of such scale
that though they were certainly interested in long-term solutions, their
immediate task was one of containment. There seems little evidence that
they feared the people of the slums in any sense other than that of increasing
social and sanitary blight; there is a good deal to suggest deep human
concern. However, the humanitarian/public health versus the repression/
control thesis may help to give future study of this question a basis in
'theory'.

The first great rupture with the voluntarist principle did not, however,
come with housing but with education. By the 1870s the voluntary system
of education had proved hopelessly inadequate in the large towns. Many
socially-minded persons who might otherwise have been 'philanthropists'
became members of the new School Boards formed under the Education
Act of 1872 which introduced general compulsory education into Scotland.
The School Board of Glasgow had achieved much in absolute terms by
1914, but it was little relative to the problem, especially as it presented
itself among the poor.

The requirement for compulsory attendance drew back and held back
the veil on the conditions of family life among the poorer classes in the
city. For it required Attendance Officers, who, if they were to do their
job at all, had to pursue delinquent children and parents into their homes,
reporting upon what they found there. It became clear that Glasgow had a
large itinerant population, flitting, often by moonlight, from one abode to
another: Attendance Officers in 1902 dealt, each week, with 450 to 500
such removals. The contrast between the large number of new, bright
and airy schools provided by the Board and the dismal homes of so many of
the pupils was dramatic: such children, indeed, lived in two distinct
worlds.

Before we can be confident about the nature of social life in Glasgow
there is much to be investigated within both the employing and the
working classes. The historical sociology of Glasgow's working classes
exists for the most part only in terms of myth and legend, some of it
apparently self-contradictory. One is told by persons of long memory that

the great tragedy was that the working classes of the city were deprived of their dignity, that essential for any fulfilment of personality. On the other hand there is the claim that the Glasgow working man was of the opinion that Jack is as good as his maister, and based his self-appraisal and his conduct upon this belief. It may be that this attitude, associated with a steel-based, heavy engineering complex, and perhaps with elements of the Calvinistic inheritance that looked askance at sentiment and refinement, produced an emphasis on virility and manhood that was very powerful, especially when confirmed by a cult of drinking. Certainly strangers to the city were astonished at the number of drunks they saw, a dingy detraction from the vigour and colour of street life.

But to understand some of the reasons why so many men had recourse to this escape, one has only to read Derick S. Thomson's poems of men from the Highlands and Islands who worked in Glasgow, but had not assimilated to the new life, whose souls hovered homeward when the concentration of work was removed, who saw dimly through the bottle things yearned for: 'Is it long that you heard from home?'

The working men and women who composed the life of Glasgow in its great heyday had their own ways of looking at life, at humanity and at God: it is dangerous and condescending to impute to them simplified views of 'class consciousness'. Their outlook was derived partly from the lives, experience and precepts of former generations. The remoter of their forebears had lived their lives in fields and among the hills; the more recent of them in the course of the industrial revolution and the generations following had been obliged to come to terms with streets and tenements, forges and factories. Like everyone else, they were to a degree prisoners of their situation, but they had their own ways of comprehending it and dealing with it that cannot be reduced to any simple pattern.

Some observers have been inclined to regard the power of the city to debase and corrupt as being without limit. Dire though the effects of urban life can be, this view of human degradation is perhaps to ignore the capacity of men and women to shape their own lives, at least in part and in some degree. Adam McNaughton, contemplating the passing of the old tenement life, recently recalled, perhaps a little sentimentally, its intensely human side:

Where is the Glasgow where I used to stay?
The white wallie close done up wi' pipe clay
Where ye knew every neighbour fae first floor to third
An' to keep your door locked was considered absurd . . .

An earlier poet of the Glasgow scene, Alexander Smith, writing as the
great prosperity was gaining momentum in the 1850s, caught the sense of
vigour and heartlessness of the city. But he ends, like McNaughton, with
the way in which men are and must be part of the place that has made
them, in spite of its ugly aspects and its sufferings:

Draw thy fierce streams of blinding ore,
Smite on a thousand anvils roar
   Down to the harbour-bars;
Smoulder in smoky sunsets, flare
On rainy nights, with street and square
   Lie empty to the stars.
From terrace proud to alley base
I know thee as my mother's face.

     *   *   *   *   *

A sacredness of love and death
Dwells in thy noise and smoky breath.

3. Civic authority

Over the life of the city there presided the Corporation of Glasgow.
It had good claim to being a 'model' of its kind, far-seeing, active,
innovatory to a degree that made it a rival, and perhaps a predominant one,
over the next most progressive British city, the Birmingham of Joseph
Chamberlain and the tradition he established there. In the spheres of
public supply of water, gas, electricity and tramways, of abattoirs,
laundries and markets, the sponsorship of the city's image through
exhibitions, the provision of Art Galleries, and in slum clearance and

urban renewal, Glasgow was a leader. In these ways Glasgow superseded Edinburgh as the Scottish show-piece of civic government, becoming a place of resort of people from many countries interested in such matters.

To attain this eminence the Corporation had used its powers with vigour. So much so that there is a suggestion of civic authoritarianism stronger than anywhere else in Britain. In so sober a journal as the *Scottish Law Review* in 1905 Glasgow Corporation was labelled 'the oppressor of the West', charged with regarding the 'Imperial Parliament as a means of registering its decrees'. There seems little doubt that Glasgow Corporation had built for itself a tradition of getting things done. In doing so it showed no fear of charges of being collectivist and bureaucratic. But that this was not to everyone's taste is clear. This was especially so in the case of adjacent boroughs, successively resisting with vigour and sometimes bitterness the city's expanding embrace.

There is evidence too that the city's magistrates and officials kept a strong hand over social discipline. This was true in the poor house. The Corporation would have no part in the sale of alcohol. In 1890 it resolved 'that no property should hereafter be let by any of the municipal departments for the purpose of carrying on the business of selling intoxicating drinks therein'. In this way the Corporation committed itself to partial local prohibition for nearly eighty years. It was hard too, on the licensees, for evangelical temperance was strongly represented on the Council. Glasgow magistrates did not hesitate to use their powers to censor art exhibitions and otherwise to preside over morality. Houses were 'ticketed' in an attempt to control overcrowding: such houses were visited without notice by Sanitary Inspectors between midnight and 4 a.m. In the streets the magistrates operated the local Police Acts with a rigour little inhibited by notions of civil liberties as they might apply to the labouring classes and to incomeless idlers. In Glasgow you could be arrested for being 'a known thief', a practice which gave the police great power. How much of the rigour of police action was due to the social values of the city's rulers, how much to a sense of social precariousness, requiring a strong hand, is a matter for interesting conjecture. But the upshot was a city in which people were safe in the streets.

Even in the great days of laissez-faire it is plain that the rulers of Glasgow took a positive, not to say assertive, view of their functions, in the provision of public facilities, in the supervision of public morality and in the preservation of public order: they combined civic activism and civic authoritarianism in a unique way.

It is perhaps not unreasonable to think of them as treating the Corporation as a kind of joint-stock company of which they were the directors, responding to the managerial challenge of city government, with the propertied classes as their shareholders. Just as in a company it was necessary to keep order and maintain discipline, so too in a city. Just as in a company the care of casualties was usually minimal, so too in municipal government. Here, again, a serious study would be rewarding. As a starting point it would be necessary to know the economic and social background of the city fathers.

4. *Social philosophy*

Social philosophy can express itself in two principal ways: in the form of proposals for amelioration, and in the form of demands for radical change. The former was the concern of the middle-class philanthropists with their emphasis upon the voluntarist principle. The latter could have roots in both the middle and working classes.

In Glasgow before 1914, middle-class intellectualism did not really converge with the working-class protest. But there was considerable middle-class radical activity. The Glasgow branch of the Socialist League was active for a time, with Bruce Glasier as its secretary: he gave impressive evidence before the housing enquiry of 1891. He was not inhibited by the fear that paralysed much thinking about housing, namely that to depart from commercially viable, self-sustaining schemes was wrong. Page Arnot was secretary of the Glasgow University Fabian Society. Tom Johnston, as a student at Glasgow University, sponsored Keir Hardie for the office of Rector, but failed; he founded and edited *Forward*, which developed an astonishing circulation for a socialist paper in Britain, largely within the Independent Labour Party. Indeed the ILP had a strong place in Glasgow, attracting men and women like John Wheatley, Emanuel Shinwell, Patrick Dollan and James Maxton, whose minds ran in terms of fundamental, though not revolutionary, change. One of the most radical of Glaswegians, the leading figure in the extreme left, was John

MacLean, a local school teacher, who lectured and agitated on vigorous Marxist lines: *Vanguard*, the organ of the Glasgow branch of the British Socialist Party, was essentially MacLean's voice. As a leader of the Glasgow revolutionary left he was ardent for the cause of republican Ireland. There was also the journalist Guy Aldred, communist, anarchist, anarcho-syndicalist, anarcho-egotist, tried and imprisoned in 1909 for a year for sedition: he was to continue active until the late 1950s.

Yet for radical ideology to take any real hold, it had to have roots in an element of the working classes. Little by way of proposals for alternative societies could be expected to come from the poor and the unskilled: effective and sustained protest had to be rooted in a group of skilled workers who felt themselves threatened with a deterioration of their condition. Such a group did not effectively appear in Glasgow, so that there was relatively little response among the workers to the intellectualism of the radical middle class, or even those who, like MacLean, had come from the working class, and little incentive to propound revolutionary solutions among themselves. The rhetoric of renovation or revolution was thus unable to find real roots in group fears or disgruntlement. In this sense the Glasgow labour movement, like that of Britain generally, would appear to have been much less affected by socialist ideas than were the workers in other European industrial countries. All this is, however, tentative: a study along such lines would yield interesting results.

5. The partial and precarious achievement

We have tried to see, in some kind of totality, the life of Glasgow from 1875 to 1914, when it was flourishing as never before and as never since. The picture is endlessly complex. But it has a kind of unity. There was a convergence of circumstances capable of producing, in mutual reinforcement, an extraordinary industrial achievement.

Some part of this is proper ground among Glaswegians for self-congratulation, or rather ancestor- or predecessor-congratulation. There is no doubt that Glasgow had its great days, that it flourished, generating gratification among its citizens and not a little admiring notice on the national and even international scene. It created also a strong and distinctive city identity. Patrick Geddes, writing in 1910, had Glasgow, along with other cities, in mind when he said, 'Every considerable city . . . seeks to complete itself . . . it finds within itself the means, and increasingly the will, to develop its own civilisation within, and not merely draws it from without'. Glasgow, more than most cities, had this capacity to produce its own ethos.

It had also, by the same processes, generated its own structure. It was a city containing enormous differences in income, class differentials that seem, in retrospect, stark indeed. But there appears to have been a minimum of class consciousness, much less overt conflict. The physical structure of the city contributed to this, for the spatial segregation of the classes was far advanced, and modes of life were thus kept distinct. The slums were highly concentrated, places so destructive of humanity that they were unlikely to produce organised and sustained protest. Housing, perhaps the greatest ground of grievance, did not provide the basis for workers' organisation or action. An effective response could only come from workers' reactions to their jobs, but no sufficiently aggrieved élite had been generated among the labour force: indeed in many cases paternalism and a common interest in the job had meant that among the men most likely to express complaints there was little such reaction to their lot. Glasgow appeared to be a contented place, partly because so many issues, though raised by an intellectual element in the city, could find no response among those thought to be aggrieved. It is an interesting conjecture whether, had labour protest been more vigorous and therefore more inhibitive upon entrepreneurship, the scale of Glasgow's growth and its commitment to heavy industry and world trade might have been less than it was.

At the root of Glasgow's existence, its triumphs in industry and commerce provided a classic case of specialised and mutually reinforcing achievement. The years of Glasgow's Victorian and Edwardian flourishing

---

3. *Shipbuilders, Whiteinch* 1899 Etching and Drypoint
Muirhead Bone found a fascination in structural shapes, especially perhaps in the shipyards. Here he suggests the cleanness of line of the hulls as they formed within the somewhat rickety-looking wooden scaffolding; he shows the men, looming large in the foreground but dwarfed in relation to the ships they are building. This is the Barclay Curle yard.

Murrhead Bone

generated a love of place and a pride in it, together with splendid buildings, a tradition of civic activism and a marvellous collectivity of skills both among managers and workers. Yet it had been obvious for a generation that certain challenges had not been met: of these the Glasgow slums were the most telling evidence.

---

4 *Drydock* 1899 Etching and Drypoint
A view of the repair yard of R. Napier and Sons. There seems to be men everywhere.

D

III. *Interlude: Wars and Depressions, 1914–45*

1. *The inheritance by 1914*

THE Glasgow of August 1914, at the levels of economic performance, urban welfare for most of the people, and general social coherence, had seemed to be functioning well, and to be set fair for the future. But in each of these aspects the city, largely inadvertently, had given heavy hostages to fortune. The economy, for all the brilliant success of its basic complex of engineering and shipbuilding, was precariously poised, depending upon the continued prosperity of world trade and the willingness of the world to have its goods and people carried by British ships. Secondly, the welfare of the city, as with all cities, was critically related to its housing: the housing stock in the city created by a combination of geographical constraints, family budgetary habits, and a free market, was to prove no longer acceptable, especially as comparisons of overcrowding and general facilities were made with other British cities: obsolescence in real terms was thus to be reinforced by a change of attitudes. Thirdly, sustained incomes and employment before 1914, together with other factors, had helped to contain social conflict, so that there had been a minimum of labour militancy.

These things – the economy, the way of life of the city, human relations in industry and the general attitude toward the prevailing social structure – were revealed after 1918, in the new condition of the world, to be in negative interaction.

2. *War, 1914–18*

In the short run, however, the First World War confirmed the classic complex of marine engineering, shipbuilding, general heavy engineering, steel and coal. Such signs as there had been that the system was precarious were to a large degree masked by the urgency of war-time demand, especially for the equipment and machinery of destruction. The revival of world trade in a brief post-war boom extended for yet a further stage the illusion of a soundly-based regional economy.

But there had come to Clydeside during the war a new labour militancy. It centred upon the Clyde Workers' Committee. The legend of Red Clyde had been born: it gained strength from 1921. It was made possible by the fact that, at long last, a sufficient grievance could be generated among the more skilled workers to give them a coherence and continuity of outlook. It centred around the phenomenon of the dilution of skilled crafts, as required by the imperatives of mass production for war purposes.

There was, too, in 1915, the Glasgow Rent Strike, a response to an attempt by the owners of house property, especially near the shipyards, to raise rents as the general price-level rose. The Rent Strike, with its tenement committees, in addition to helping to cause the government to bring in war-time rent control through the Rent Restriction Act, thus provided a housing parallel to industrial militancy. But this aspect of protest was unable to survive: working class solidarity proved much more difficult in housing than in industry.

3. Labour, housing and politics, 1918–39

Throughout the 'twenties there was never less than 14 per cent of the insured labour force of Scotland out of work. In the 1930s world trade, the element upon which Clydeside had come to rest so much of its existence, virtually collapsed. Throughout that decade unemployment in the west of Scotland averaged more than 25 per cent. The effects on output were catastrophic: that of pig iron was reduced to one-third and the local coalmines and shipyards produced at scarcely more than half their pre-war levels in the later part of the decade. The commitment to heavy engineering and to international trade had produced a reversal of fortune so complete as to be paralysing. The result was idle men on street corners, as Iain Crichton-Smith described them, 'chewing the fag-ends of a failed culture'.

The ballet *Miracle in the Gorbals*, with its depiction of unemployment and poverty, set the image of Glasgow for Englishmen. It was reinforced by the novel *No Mean City* of 1935 by Alexander MacArthur and K. Long. The razor gangs described in it were a reflection of economic breakdown – they were composed of grown men, not youths; they were adults reacting to unemployment, poverty and boredom. They did not divide on ethnic or sectarian lines, and were no real threat to the general public but only to one another. The gangs were in a sense a surface phenomenon; the Gorbals was a true community, assimilating a succession of immigrant groups – Irish, Jews, Lithuanians, bringing colour, and perhaps coherence. The Gorbals gangs were less formidable than those of the east end, where history and ideology of a sort entered: the Billy Boys of Bridgeton boasted that they could raise 400 men. There were also the Sally Boys, the Norman Conks and the Baltic Fleet.

There was, too, by the 1930s, the problem of Glasgow's reputation for labour unrest, as it became embedded in the minds of business men and the general public elsewhere. Notoriety for strikes and political radicalism came suddenly, but with crippling completeness. It began with the 'Labour Withholding Committee' during the War, and came to a climax with the Forty Hour Strike in 1919, culminating in a riot in George Square. Enormous publicity was given to the latter event: there was etched upon the public mind of Britain a picture of a close-packed crowd of men in cloth caps, a red flag rising in their midst so shortly after the Russian revolution. The police dispersed the demonstrators with a baton charge, adding further drama to the incident. The conception of Glasgow thus inspired was ineradicable. But there was a reality behind it. Socialism in Glasgow had found a solid base in groups of worried and frustrated workers, and on this the shop stewards and the Labour Withholding Committee had built. Skilled men had seen the differential upon which their self-respect rested shrink as the labour force was diluted; to this was added the ultimate insult of unemployment as shipyards and engineering works fell silent. The yards either closed completely or took a few loss-making contracts in order to maintain as much as they could of their skilled labour pool.

The Glasgow economy, the root of its social problems, could only be changed by profound structural alteration, sponsored and largely financed by government, aided by a revival of world trade and of the British economy as one of the most important elements within it. But there was no experience anywhere of such an operation by the state. How was the regional economy to be apprehended so that the necessary changes might be identified? The elements of the industry of the west of Scotland stood in an organic relationship to one another, for this was the basis on which they had been created. Business organisation and outlook, and the skills of the labour force, were both specific to the conditions that had produced them. There was no obvious programme either for the amputation of old industries or the engraftment of new ones.

But the political process could not stand still. Vigorous party politics had entered Glasgow civic government. In 1933, in the depth of depression, the Labour Party displaced the traditional unstructured, middle class kind of rule. It was to continue in power until the present day, except for two brief intervals totalling five years. In the General Election of 1922 the Labour Party scored a spectacular triumph in Glasgow, winning two-thirds of its seats, a striking political portent.

The intention of the Labour Party was to ease the condition of the workers in times so desperate for so many. But Glasgow Corporation, like the national government, found it hard indeed to establish a policy formula. It could attempt minor measures in areas over which it had some control, for example the inclusion of 'fair wages' clauses in municipal contracts, and the setting up of a direct labour department to do building and other work on a 'socialist' basis for the city. But it could do so little to revive local industry so that the fundamental problems of incomes and jobs might be dealt with. It also became aware that spending on industrial development in the absence of central government aid would push up the rates and so act as a deterrent to business.

The political confrontation in Glasgow has always been harsher than in England. The Scottish Independent Labour Party had a strong revolutionary element, whereas the English Independent Labour Party was largely reformist. But the Clydeside M.P.s achieved relatively little in Parliament. Partly this was because they could provide no effective programme for 'socialism in one city'. Even more fundamental, once out of their own atmosphere, they saw the world in wider terms. They were not the first or the last to find that issues that had produced absolutes in a local context lost their simplicity when seen as part of a larger whole; the obsessional and mutually confirming clarity that could develop in the côteries, the committee rooms and the emotional public meetings of Glasgow dissolved into relativities when carried to Westminster. This process was aided by the atmosphere of the House of Commons and the urbanities displayed there.

Failing a policy for industrial development, the Corporation turned to attempts to improve social conditions, especially by means of programmes of subsidised housing. This meant, of course, looking to the central government for financial help, and making housing a social service. The programme of house building was begun under a Conservative or 'Moderate' Town Council, using powers under the Addison Act of 1919, under which large central government subsidies were provided: the Housing Department was founded in that year. But the local authority liability was limited to the product of a penny rate. It was a Glasgow M.P., John Wheatley (representing Shettleston), who, as Minister of Health in the first Labour government in 1924, carried a Housing Act which provided additional subsidies for local authority housing, on condition the houses were rented and not sold; the Corporation thus gained greater power to tackle housing on a real scale. So it was that Glasgow, even without a Labour Council until 1933, developed an ever-increasing commitment to house building; low rents and subsidy were entered upon by a Conservative local administration, with consequent implications for local taxation through the rates.

Under the Housing Acts of 1919, 1923, and 1924 the Conservatives in Glasgow built several housing estates on open ground on the periphery of the city, the largest being Mosspark and Knightswood, as well as building on sites within the city. The theoretical basis of a policy of housing estates was, of course, that by thus beginning well up the social and income scale, the new housing areas would add to the amenity of the city, at the same time releasing houses vacated by the more fortunate for occupancy by those who were less so.

The Corporation, ruled by the 'Moderates', took its tenants for the green-field developments on a selective basis; they were largely skilled and semi-skilled men and white-collar workers, to the exclusion of the dwellers in the slums. This represented, in effect, a continuance of nineteenth and early twentieth century policies of assisting the 'deserving', those who could most 'benefit' from their new homes.

There was at first a reaction against tenements in the case of the new areas, for they had become associated in the Corporation's mind with bad housing: the result was large estates consisting, uncharacteristically, of cottages and flatted houses, with a good deal of garden space. But there was a return to tenement style in the 1920s, especially in the rehousing areas.

Knightswood, built between 1923 and 1929, was the largest of the inter-war housing schemes. It was intended to be a model of its kind, and was indeed a show-piece for the city, with its generous open space, its social centre, library and seven parades of shops. The result of this policy was communities that were middle class in outlook to a high degree. And yet the schemes came to contain a fair degree of voting power for Labour, especially when, from 1933 onward, the Corporation was in Labour hands with its policy of cheap, subsidised, rented housing. This was partly because a significant number who lived in the schemes had become 'municipal Men', members of the forty thousand or so who worked for the Corporation in its many functions. Such people, living in a scheme house with its subsidy, and enjoying secure civic employment, were largely insulated from the fluctuations of the market economy. It was not surprising that for all their respectability, their votes were in some measure cast to help to determine their own rents and earnings and to ensure their own employment. Equally, it was to be expected, under depression conditions, that workers not thus protected resented the security of the Corporation's employees.

In other areas the policy followed was quite different: to some degree this was necessarily so. The sites were nearer the centre of the city, with adjacent gasworks, industry and railway lines. Blackhill, where 980 new houses were built in the 1930s, exemplified the problem. It was not long before serious deterioration had taken place, the inevitable outcome of lack of social coherence compounded by deprivation and demoralisation. Those growing up in the Glasgow of the later 'thirties recall that it was not the Gorbals, with its communal identity and social mix, that they feared to walk through, but Blackhill. In part Blackhill came to represent, perhaps by inadvertence, a solution proposed by various reformers before 1914, namely the segregation of the socially difficult: it served, however, to produce a new situation worse in many respects than the old. It is not clear how the Blackhill situation came about; perhaps some historian of the city will tell us. It seems most probable that the development was planned in terms of minimal cost, in order to keep down the rents; if so, this might well have meant that a population of low-income tenants would contain a disproportionate element of anti-social families; the character of the area would thereafter be self-confirming as those seeking betterment moved out and were replaced by problem families.

There were thus two principal kinds of development in Glasgow – new and well-furbished estates on empty agricultural land round the perimeter, and other sites where no real new beginning was possible, and where old problems were ominously perpetuated and compounded.

The Corporation had learned by 1939, in both the Knightswood and Mosspark schemes, and in Blackhill, that the provision of subsidised housing, in addition to having profound implications for the rates, also involved it in determining the social structure of component parts of the city. With free market pricing for houses replaced by control and subsidy, the only alternative was rationing, making the Corporation the arbiter between the claims of families and of social classes. This 'control' became an aspect of the functioning of the Housing Department. In Birmingham and other English cities at this time private builders were constructing outer rings of 'modern semis' to be sold to eager buyers.

But there could be no turning back; in spite of the vigour of the interwar housing programme, Glasgow's problem remained acute; as one deeply concerned councillor put it, 'Give us the houses and to hell with planning'. Such a remark was inspired by a compelling sense of urgency. But it perhaps also reflected an outlook described by the Scottish Architectural Advisory Committee in 1935, that 'an absence of gardens, a sombre and unlovely exterior and overcrowded conditions . . . normal to Scottish working-class housing' had produced a concentration on the internal aspects of housing, with a corresponding indifference to externals, including appearance, community planning, spacing and the exploitation of topographical advantages.

Yet considerable housing progress was made. Between 1919 and 1939, 76,360 houses were authorised to be built in the city: of these 54,289 were Corporation houses and 10,235 had state assistance. Only 9,106 were privately built, so that Glasgow housing swung violently in the direction of public ownership. But in another sense the old tradition continued: Glasgow remained a city of small houses, building in the inter-war years only 29·0 per cent of houses with four rooms or more, against an average for England and Wales of 80·3 per cent.

4. The search for industrial solutions

In the industrial sphere there were initiatives from the business men, including the formation of the Scottish National Development Council, and the building of the Hillington Industrial Estate and other smaller ones. Both were intended to promote industrial diversification. But those who, like Sir Stephen (later Lord) Bilsland, sought to create a strong leadership from the Glasgow business community, though they had some successes, were unable to mobilise business interest in regional recovery to any great degree. An attempt in 1938, sponsored by Glasgow's Union Bank, under Bilsland and Norman Hird, to persuade the Scottish banks to join in a Scottish Development Finance Corporation, failed. It may have been the case, indeed, that the potential for collective action by business men was severely limited.

The great problem of the inter-war years for Glasgow business men was how to carry out rationalisation so that redundant and out of date plant could be scrapped and production concentrated upon the most efficient units. This was especially necessary in the two great sectors of steel and shipbuilding. It was a fundamentally different challenge from the competitive demands of the later nineteenth century: it called for co-operation rather than competition. The story is a fascinating but sad one. It proved very difficult, given the personalities involved, and the varied and often conflicting interests of the firms which they headed, to restructure these two basic industries to the degree required. The government recoiled from using coercion – indeed it felt that with the expertise in the hands of the steel and shipbuilding masters, only they could carry out the task. But these men were caught up in historically determined relationships that made a co-operative reorganisation of their industries a painful operation. Some degree of success was, however, achieved in both sectors. Rearmament from the later 'thirties helped the recovery of these industries.

Two figures perhaps dominated the Clydeside industrial scene in these inter-war years. There was Lord Weir and, especially, Sir James Lithgow. The latter was the head of the shipbuilding firm on the lower Clyde at Port Glasgow that bore his family name. He was perhaps the last of the masters in the heavy industries cast in the heroic mould, chairman of the Shipbuilding Employers' Federation when he was thirty-seven.

In the early 'thirties he was a rich man, head of a viable shipyard with a healthy balance sheet. But he could not fail to be aware of the condition of two of the greatest of Glasgow firms, Beardmore's and Fairfield's. Both were in the deepest trouble, in debt to the banks and in imminent danger of collapse. As early as the later 1920s Lithgow had visited Montagu Norman, Governor of the Bank of England, with proposals for rationalising the British shipbuilding industry. Lithgow was one of the few who approached the Governor not to beg, but from a strong personal position, with constructive ideas. These coincided with Norman's own thinking and his experience of Vickers, Armstrong, Baldwin's, Beardmore's, etc. The result of these talks was the setting up in 1930 of the National Shipbuilders Security with Lithgow as chairman.

But Beardmore's and Fairfield's were in so bad a state as to require special treatment. The Bank had taken up most of the issue of the first debenture stock of Beardmore's in order to avoid collapse. Norman had great difficulty in finding able management for broken-down firms: he turned to Lithgow. In 1932 Lithgow became involved in Beardmore's and in 1934 with Fairfield's.

In the case of Beardmore's the balance sheet was heavily overcapitalised: one of the great problems was how to service so large a capital, much increased as it had been between 1914 and 1918. Norman needed a buyer who would take over the stock held by the Bank of England, Lloyds and Lord Invernairn (William Beardmore). This Sir James and his brother Henry did at an agreed price, taking the risk of collapse, and assuming the management. By this time, in the later 1930s, rearmament was beginning. But it is doubtful if the Lithgows made much out of the recovery and the war-time prosperity, for most of the profits were ploughed back into the firm. The Lithgows also took over Fairfield's in a similar way. (They had, moreover, taken a large interest in Colville's in 1934.) These were the first of the great Clydeside rescue operations, carried out by two west of Scotland business men in co-operation with the Bank of England. The motives of James and Henry Lithgow were largely altruistic, based upon the feeling that they had a duty to try to support industry and employment in the west of Scotland. They were successful because of the new and effective management they introduced, together with a recovery of markets. (The Lithgow interest in Colville's and Beardmore's ended when these firms were nationalised in 1950; their Fairfield stake was virtually destroyed when that firm went into crisis in 1965.)

But no figures of the stature of the Lithgows appeared in the newer sectors of Glasgow industry, capable of bringing the much needed diversification.

5. The Glasgow way of life

In spite of Glasgow's many troubles, and of the changes it underwent, the city continued to generate a distinctive style of life, on the memories of which the nostalgia of the older generation of its citizens is based. Its principal celebrants have been Jack House and Cliff Hanley, with their recollections of the Glasgow of their youth in the 'twenties and 'thirties. There was the Highland-man's Umbrella (the enormous railway bridge leading over Argyle Street to Central Station, forming the largest pend in Glasgow with built-in shops and bars), where was nightly to be found the strongest concentration of the Gaelic tongue in the world, the spontaneous centre of the metropolis of Gaeldom. There was the Alhambra and other theatres (of which there were eleven in the 1930s), where Glaswegians passed their own kind of comment on the performances. There were the cinemas that had proliferated in Glasgow as in every western city, vast and warm, darkened shrines where the people of one culture were exposed to the dream-world of another, though as they queued for admission they were entertained by buskers, products of their own reality. There were the double-ender ferries (that could 'go backwards and forwards without turnin' round', and were free), and the Glasgow Underground with its authentic earthy smell; there were summer trips by tram to Queen's Park and Rouken Glen. There were the great shipyards ranked along the Clyde, and 'the Barras' at the centre of things, one of the few street markets in Scotland ('a day at the barras' was an adventure). There was the obsession with football (offering an escape for a gifted few from the rut of industrial employment or unemployment). There was a more than average ration of lurid murder, together with the campaign by Sillitoe, the Chief Constable, against the razor gangs. As a brave attempt to reassert the greatness of

Glasgow's past, the Empire Exhibition of 1938 drew its denizens to Bellahouston Park.

These things generated a working class folk lore, centred upon the tenements, often confirmed and projected by music hall and pantomime songs and jokes. The factor (the owner's agent and rent collector) was a favourite figure of derision, collecting his rents, ignoring the bugs behind the wallpaper and complaining that the coal bunker has been chopped up yet again. Games in streets and on middens, infant terrors of going in the dark to the toilet far from the safety of home, women taking turns cleaning the stairs, the 'jawbox' (the kitchen sink) with its multiple uses, visits to the pawnshop – these were the things of which much of life was composed, elements of a shared culture on which a humour of self deprecation and hidden rancour could be based. It was a humour of false teeth and corsets and bunions, reflecting excessive sugar consumption with lack of dental care, a heavy carbohydrate diet, and ill-fitting shoes.

The working class culture of the traditional Glasgow tenements is very inadequately recorded. In spite of families that were individualist, both in terms of respectability and social outrageousness, it was a group culture, setting strong limits outside which you did not step, or at least took care not to be seen to step. The improvement of self and family were too often looked upon as pretension. This was especially compelling and limiting in education. Bright schoolboys doing conspicuously well in class could have a difficult time, slanged by their schoolmates. With girls the constraints were even more drastic for they were expected to marry and subordinate themselves to their families. To make way in such a situation the home had to be insulated from the rest of the world: this in itself could add to the claustrophobia of a family bent upon improving the prospects of its children.

6. *War resumed, 1939–45*

With the coming of the Second World War it was as though fate had revived the conditions of Clydeside's great days before 1914, posing an insatiable demand for the things in which she had excelled in late Victorian and Edwardian times. War demand mopped up the 178,000 work-people who had begun to think of themselves as useless, and brought new capital investment into industry that had so shortly before been regarded as cursed with hopelessly excess capacity.

Such tentative steps as there had been in bringing structural change to the industries of the west of Scotland were submerged in the rush to refurbish, once again, a pattern that was now appropriate only to war, and to war with its technological base in heavy industry. The north-western sea approaches to Britain became important once more under the threat of German submarines: Glasgow became again a cosmopolitan city, one of the great links between Europe and America. Something of the pre-1914 prosperity and sense of success returned.

But much irreversible change had occurred. The state had shouldered great burdens: the basis of the welfare state had been provided and a policy of regional economic development was emerging. Housing had become to a considerable degree a subsidised social service, and the private sector had been brought under rent control. In the potential of all of these changes, Glasgow had a great interest. Yet, in spite of such programmes of amelioration, the experience of the inter-war years had profoundly affected trade union development and labour outlook: in industry and in local and national government the claims of labour in Glasgow, as in the rest of Britain, were now much more potent.

IV. *The Faltering Economy 1945–75*

1. *Partial revival, 1945–60*

WITH the coming of peace in 1945, it seemed to many that Glasgow, with her heavy industrial base confirmed by war, would return to the agonies of the 'thirties. But in the years from 1945 to the late 1950s, matters turned out quite differently. The war-time boost to the industries of the region had brought a degree of rethinking in management, and a greater under-standing on the part of government in its relations with industry. Under the conditions of war, knowledge and skill had been gaining in the manipulation of the economy as a whole, and of regional elements within it. Keynesian ideas for the maintenance of effective demand had become government policy. The world economy, once the austere years immedi-ately following the war had passed, entered upon a phase of prosperity extraordinary in its level and persistence.

In this recovery and expansion Glasgow and the west of Scotland shared. For some fifteen years after 1945 the region, in common with the country as a whole, had low levels of unemployment, marvellously different from the desperate years of the 'thirties. There was little sign indeed of the curse of the inter-war years; there were few men who were permanently unemployed.

But expectations too had changed. Whereas Keynes had thought an economy could scarcely operate with less than about 5 per cent unemploy-ment, Britain in these years had pushed the figure below 2 per cent. This meant that in comparative terms the performance of the west of Scotland was poor, with unemployment averaging 3 to 3·5 per cent, or approaching twice that of Britain as a whole. This level of unemployment that would have been unimaginably low in the 'thirties, and indeed in industrial history generally, was now taken as a ground of failure and recrimination. The Scottish trades unions could not accept so invidious a comparison with the rest of the United Kingdom. The planners were challenged to obtain an employment figure of 98 per cent. This was to pose a virtually insoluble problem, especially in the light of the economic structure of Glasgow and the west. But it could supply the basis for labour militancy in some industries.

Such an approach does not take account of two further factors. The first of these was emigration: the west of Scotland lost about three-quarters of its natural increase in the 'sixties, so that its labour force grew only slightly, staying at more or less a million. In this respect, as with unemployment, general attitudes changed with relative success: it became less and less acceptable that so high a proportion of the young should be obliged to seek employment outside the region.

Secondly, per capita incomes in Glasgow and the west fell behind the national average, being something like 10 per cent lower. This was reflected in, among other things, a much smaller proportionate car population, though Glasgow's relative shortage of cars was partly the result of the highly concentrated form of the city. Even so, Scottish Gross Domestic Product had grown by nearly 60 per cent, though that of Britain had increased by 70 per cent.

In the years from the end of the war to the 'sixties, then, in general economic terms, though there were demands that unemployment be brought down to the national average, that means be found of generating additional jobs so as to arrest emigration, and, to some extent, that income levels of the west of Scotland be raised to those of Britain as a whole, the picture was not too bad. Certainly there was concern about these matters, as various enquiries, including the Toothill Report of 1961, showed. Social conditions in Glasgow further deteriorated in many ways. But, in general, Glasgow, especially in terms of incomes and employment relative to the inter-war years, was flourishing, riding the wave of British and world prosperity.

2. The collapse of the classic industries

But there were other aspects to the situation, largely veiled in the 'fifties, that became increasingly apparent in the 'sixties and early 'seventies. Conditions external to Britain were changing in an irrevocable way: her share of world trade and of shipbuilding was rapidly diminishing. Clydeside was thus confronted with creeping obsolescence on a massive scale. In

regional terms, the old structural problem deriving from Victorian and
Edwardian times was still there. The upas tree of heavy engineering had
killed or discouraged the growth of other industries of a more modern
kind beneath its massive and intertwined branches; now the upas tree itself,
so long ailing, was decaying, its limbs falling away one by one. Not only
had it been inimical to other growths, it had, by an inversion of its condition before 1914, brought about limitation of its own performance.

The chilling fact became apparent that even in its traditional sectors,
once the basis of its pride, Clydeside industry was doing less well than were
other areas of Britain. Shipbuilding on the Clyde had reached a point of
crisis. So too had locomotive building (North British Locomotive, after
prolonged struggles, ceased production in 1963). The making of machine
tools was in sad decline. In chemicals, the old Glasgow ascendancy had
totally disappeared; Tennant's Stalk was felled and the site of the St. Rollox
works became a high-rise housing development. The ending of Dixon's
Blazes removed from the scene a celebrated iron works. Reciprocally,
Glasgow and the west had drawn to itself too little of the new industries,
especially automobiles and electronics. There was a failure, either
spontaneously or with government aid, either to regenerate the old, or to
cause a sufficient structural shift from the old to the new.

There were, indeed, some valiant attempts to remake older firms. In
shipbuilding, for example, Barclay Curle and Co., after a consideration of
their position, decided to specialise in the building of short-distance
passenger ships, a reasonable enough programme at the time, but one
which failed to anticipate the massive growth of air travel. Fairfield's
adopted a policy of investment and modernisation, with a view to building
one passenger and one naval ship per year, but again the demand assumptions were not borne out. The failure of these companies to renew themselves were thus, in the main, failures in market assessment. North British
Locomotive tried to move from steam to diesel, using the Voith hydraulic
transmission from Germany. There were serious technical difficulties.
These were followed by the decision by British Rail to adopt an electrical

---

5. *Kingston Rag Store* (detail) 1899 Drypoint
Glasgow women, wearing shawls, with their bundles of rags and clothing for
sale to the store. The trade still goes on, though it no longer serves, as in the
past, as a vehicle for the typhus-bearing flea.

Wood Lane

transmission. The failure of North British would thus seem to have been due to a combination of technical defect and of rejection by the largest element in the market. In such industries, where very large indivisible decisions had to be made, and where public money was not available, error was both likely and costly, with a high probability of being fatal.

Little or no serious effort has been made to extract the meaning of past industrial experience, through the study of the striking cases of failure to adapt that have occurred in West Central Scotland. In case after case great enterprises have failed, adding nothing to any general framework of analysis relevant to policy, that might make other firms more effective, or provide guidance when an injection of public money is proposed.

3. Crisis on the Upper Clyde

It was in shipbuilding, of course, that industrial crisis on Clydeside took its most dramatic form.

John Brown's, perhaps the most famous of all British yards, had persisted in building great liners of the kind that had made her famous, and upon which the labour-intensive finishing trades depended. But inflation was carrying costs, especially wages, upward at a disastrous rate: the splendid *Kungsholm* cost £7 m. and was eventually delivered for £4 m. The *Queen Elizabeth II* ran into one difficulty after another, including labour stoppages, so that relations between John Brown's and the Cunard Company became very strained. Cash crisis was endemic.

As some shipyards closed and as others found their difficulties increasing, there were half-hearted attempts to find formulae for amalgamation. By 1962 most yards were losing money.

In 1965 Fairfield's suffered a financial collapse, posing a problem for government, private enterprise and the unions. Under the leadership of Iain Stewart, a leading Glasgow industrialist, the Fairfield (Glasgow) Ltd.

---

6. *Wood Lane* 1899 Drypoint
Good tenements from the early nineteenth century, here degenerated into slums.

E

experiment was begun in 1966, with finance from all three sources. The intention was to make a new beginning in Clydeside shipbuilding, with Fairfield's as a pacesetter and laboratory. The unions participated, but Clydeside shipbuilders generally stood aloof. Some notable successes were achieved, including the modernisation of techniques, the reduction of restrictive practices, the improvement of industrial relations, the introduction of better management techniques, and improved wages. But other firms were by now in serious difficulty. These were aggravated by the fact that Fairfield wage levels had been extended to the other yards.

The yards of the Upper Clyde could either struggle on separately, with Yarrow's with its naval contracts the only one viable, or there could be a merger on which basis a rationalisation could be attempted. In 1967 the Geddes Committee recommended a general amalgamation on the Upper Clyde. The Labour government, under strong pressure from the unions, and worried about its traditional stronghold in the west of Scotland, agreed to provide finance for a new concern. It would include John Brown, Yarrow, Connell, Fairfield and Alexander Stephen, a highly varied collection, very difficult to co-ordinate. Together they employed some 14,000 men, over a quarter of all British shipbuilding workers outside the naval dockyards. At least twice that number of workers in other engineering trades relied on the yards, and a further important element beyond them. Early in 1968 Upper Clyde Shipbuilders was formed, and took over the five yards. The Fairfield experiment, as a separate venture, came to an end, making a judgement of it very difficult. By March 1970 the government had advanced £20·2 m. in grants and loans in this rescue operation.

There were those who said that the money, or part of it, should have been given to the more efficient builders, Scott Lithgow of the Lower Clyde, working without the constraints of a narrow river, employing some 10,500 men. But the workers of the Upper Clyde, with their tradition and pride, their local community and their homes, were unwilling to migrate or commute lower down the river. The workers in all the constituent yards of UCS demanded and got rates on a parity with the best-paying yards.

The labour force was slimmed to some degree and some rationalisation was attempted. But labour relations were not good; the strike record rivalled that of the motor industry. Yarrow's, with its concentration on warships (including foreign ones), resumed its independence in 1971. A liquidator was appointed for UCS in June 1971. It seemed as though shipbuilding on the Upper Clyde was at last to undergo truly drastic diminution.

But the issue was more politically sensitive than ever. The Labour government had been replaced by a Conservative one, and though the latter had desperately few votes to lose in the west of Scotland, it was unwilling to accept the opprobrium of allowing UCS to collapse. Moreover, in July the workers, led by James Reid and James Airlie, both Communists, launched a 'work-in'. The men occupied the yards and continued to work on the jobs in hand, being paid by the liquidator out of UCS assets. The cry was that all jobs must be saved, later generalised to 'the right to work'.

There were governmental fears of serious disturbance in Glasgow. Mr. Heath's Conservative administration, already shocked by the failure of Rolls-Royce in 1970, made a U-turn in the direction of direct support of enterprises in difficulty, abandoning its former principle of refusing to aid 'lame ducks'. In this way the Conservative Party joined the Labour Party in a policy of massive support for ailing industries, beginning in Glasgow.

The government came to the conclusion that two yards were viable, namely Govan (formerly Fairfield's) and Linthouse (formerly Stephen's): Govan Shipbuilders was formed in September 1971 to replace UCS; it had Scotstoun Marine (formerly the Connell yard) as a subsidiary. Government money was provided to the extent of £35 m. This left the old John Brown yard, perhaps the least efficient and the most militant. In August 1972 it passed to Marathon Manufacturing of Houston, Texas for £1·5 m., together with promised government support of £12 m. It would build oil platforms for the North Sea, though the legs would have to be fitted lower down the Clyde below the new Erskine Bridge. The workers promised no strikes for four years, a pledge that has been kept.

By the end of 1975, £101 m. of public money had been committed in grants and loans to attempt to rehabilitate shipbuilding on the Upper Clyde. It consisted of £30 m. to Upper Clyde Shipbuilders, £59·4 m. to Govan Shipbuilders and £12 m. to Marathon Shipbuilding. So immense a sum could have built a superlative new yard, better located, or could have been used in directions other than shipbuilding. But so great was the power of continuity, as expressed in workers' attitudes and in the outlook of governments as they sought to maintain their standing and to avoid unrest, that this element of industry could still draw to itself immense resources.

It is hardly surprising that Govan Shipbuilders should be known locally as Treasure Island.

Yet what was a government faced with such a situation to do? The world market for ships had shrunk, and other countries had low wages and high subsidies. Strong feeling, not to say passion, had been aroused in Glasgow and a powerful and effective protest organisation existed. On the economic side, it was extremely difficult to arrive at the scale and nature of what was required to make the Clydeside shipbuilding industry viable. Public money, doled out at successive crises, was the response of successive governments.

4. *The regional attempt at a new industrial base: steel and automobiles*

Well before the classic industries entered upon crisis, it had become apparent that a new industrial initiative was called for in the west of Scotland. The lesson of excessive specialisation had been, in a sense, learned: 'imbalance' was seen as the condition to be remedied, and diversification as the principal aim of policy. The two elements around which it was thought a solution might be built were steel and the automobile.

It was necessary by the mid-'fifties to rethink the position in terms of steel, for much of the Scottish plant was now small and out of date in terms of modern technology, unable to reap the benefits of continuous production. Great changes had taken place in steel technology since 1945, making possible enormous improvements in productivity. To take advantage of these the first fully integrated steel mill in Scotland was built at Ravenscraig between 1951 and 1957. But matters did not stand still. By the time Ravenscraig was in operation a new steel debate had been going on for several years, centred upon the idea of a single British fully integrated strip steel mill, of one million tons capacity. But where was this employment generator to be? The debate was overtaken by the recession of 1957–8. The Scottish Trades Union Congress pressed that there should be not one major but two lesser mills, one in Scotland. The Conservative government adopted this view: Scotland received one of two semi-automated hot-strip mills at Ravenscraig, together with a cold-reduction plant at Gartcosh. Colville's could not finance this development on its own, and was given a £50 m. loan by the government. Scottish steel production was thus increased between 1947 and 1960 from 1 million tons to 2·7 million.

Shortly afterwards, in the early 1960s, it proved possible to interest the Rootes Group in establishing a car plant at Linwood, near Glasgow, in conjunction with Pressed Steel Fisher (taken over by Rootes in 1966). There thus seemed to be the possibility that the Scottish steel industry could be remade, with a secure market for its increased output in a major west of Scotland automobile plant, specialising in a new small car (the Imp) with good market potential, together with prospects for light plate for shipbuilding.

These projects in steel and automobiles were backed by public policy, using the full range of national and regional incentives. They constituted the basis of a strategy for industrial renewal. At Linwood the local authorities and the Scottish Office collaborated to provide houses, roads and general facilities: a new community was brought into being. The Rootes plant was opened in 1963: by 1975 some £45 m. had been invested in it.

It was hoped that from these policies would come self-sustaining economic growth: indeed a state of euphoria was engendered among many. The Linwood scheme had powerful backing from the Scottish trade union movement. But there were those who doubted, arguing on a cost–benefit basis, that, even under the most favourable assumptions, the Linwood scheme would never be able to pay its way.

The Rootes Group was in serious trouble by 1967. In that year it sold a majority interest to the Chrysler Corporation of America, who at the same time bought the Simca plant in France, thus taking a double stake in Europe. Labour relations were bad in an undertaking that was already competitively precarious. All too soon conditions were such that a man who had done his apprenticeship, acquiring his skills and anxious to use them, could be frustrated by being so often called out on strike, and so would go elsewhere. There were some 300 stoppages between 1963 and 1969. But labour relations improved in the 1970s, so that in 1974 the Scottish automobile industry had a splendid record compared with the English Midlands or Merseyside. Nevertheless Chrysler were unwilling to sink more money into the Linwood venture, to modernise and introduce new models. Late in 1975 the government, under powerful political pressure, intervened, supplying new money, but agreeing with Chrysler on a programme of slimming involving heavy redundancies.

By this time Scottish steel too was again in grave difficulties, requiring further modernisation and an accompanying reduction in the labour force if it was to remain competitive.

The fundamental strategy for the renewal of the industrial base of the west of Scotland was thus called in question by events. In part the programme was a casualty of the crisis confronting the British car industry generally, and in part the relative failure derived from specific Scottish conditions. The auxiliary industries it was hoped to attract were unwilling to move north on a sufficient scale.

It could be argued that the entire Linwood scheme was shaky even at its conception, and ought not to have been undertaken. But, given a set of circumstances that might have yielded success, it is difficult to see what other general course could have been followed. Conversely, it is easy to sympathise with the optimism which, in the face of warnings, pushed the scheme through, carrying the government with it, hoping that serendipity would produce unforeseen benefits.

Meanwhile the concentration of industry had been proceeding. By 1968 in the Clydeside conurbation the 100 largest manufacturing *plants* employed more than 50 per cent of all manufacturing workers; the 100 largest *enterprises* (some with two or more plants) accounted for over 70 per cent. Thus nearly three-quarters of the labour force in manufacturing were employed by 100 firms. With the continuance of the trend to concentration, this controlling number has become even fewer.

5. The quality of private management

How far has the poor performance of Clydeside industry been the responsibility of management? The quality of management in Glasgow and the west has been a matter of much debate. It is notoriously difficult in this field to establish sound criteria of performance that allow of comparison and general conclusions. The response necessary to remake a decaying firm in a declining industry may be very much higher than might be needed to create a new enterprise in an expanding, high profit sector; the partial success of the former may represent a higher level of managerial performance than the resounding triumphs of the latter.

Any assessment of the quality of management involves a scrutiny of the choice of aims of the enterprise, the means available for their attainment, and the effectiveness with which means are used to serve ends: in all three respects scrutiny is difficult. Little serious research has been attempted into Clydeside industries along these lines. The firm histories that have emerged from Glasgow and its region have had almost no analytical bite. The Scottish Business School founded in 1971, involving the universities of Glasgow, Edinburgh and Strathclyde, has perhaps not had time to enter into the problem of rehabilitating the region in business terms; the question arises, however, whether the attributes of business imagination, judgment and courage can be taught.

Perhaps most serious of all, in the short run, the authors of the West Central Scotland Plan of 1974, in providing so much of what was needed to understand the region, made no real effort to penetrate industry in this way; they failed to seek an understanding of management performance, and indeed of the performance of firms. In the absence of such information it is difficult to know which firms should receive public backing, in what form, to what degree, and on what terms.

On *a priori* grounds, however, it would seem not unlikely that, with so little participation in the growth sectors of British industry, Glasgow has generated or attracted less than its share of innovative and imaginative management. The amenity reputation of the city may also have had its effect in this regard. The shift-share analysis carried out for the West Central Scotland Plan would seem to point to at least some degree of management failure.

There was, too, the long-continued but increasing tendency for the concentration of certain business functions in London and the south, especially those requiring face-to-face contact, including marketing, finance and research development: these may have caused a degree of movement of higher management away from the provincial cities to the national metropolis. A good many of the great firms of Scotland have indeed undergone this kind of shift, including Burmah Oil, Collins the publishers and the Distillers Company. Most, including the aforementioned, strive, however, to retain as much as possible of their Scottish character: moreover, this relationship with London may well have the effect of broadening Scottish business outlook and experience. The London offices of the Scottish banks certainly act as a means of participating in a larger business world, of which the banks have made valuable use. Improvements in Glasgow's air flight links with London, especially after the opening of Abbotsinch Airport in 1966, may have done something to arrest the drain of business talent; the Glasgow–London service is the busiest internal route in Europe.

But the tendency remains strong, in all economies, for a centralising of the information and contact net. In this sense the quality and incentives of management, together with the range of decisions available to it, are problems affecting *all* provincial cities. They can have a cultural as well as a physical aspect. It may be that Scottish firms should give continuous thought to this problem so that the balance of management does not drift southward by inadvertence.

The effectiveness of management and labour are, of course, interdependent. Over a considerable range of functions, management in both public and private sectors within a free society can only be as efficient as labour permits it to be. If labour is ossifying, refusing to learn new tasks, or is excessively militant, management, being largely composed of a professional, non-owning class, will try to work within the conditions thus set, and will, indeed, have little alternative but to connive in reducing the effectiveness of the concern, as long as market conditions or subsidy make this possible. Evidence of this occurring on Clydeside is not lacking; in much of the east of Scotland there seems to have been a more constructive atmosphere. Together workers and management determine efficiency, and, in large measure, the surplus which in turn largely governs new investment and modernisation.

It is no good yearning for a return of the age of the tycoons of Victorian times, for management is now a very different function, to be carried on in very different conditions. Similarly, though regional loyalty may still play an important part, it is no longer possible to think of management as a locally raised product, bound to its place of origin. As with a football team, talent must be sought where it is to be found, it must be attracted by free choice, and it must be paid for on the appropriate scale. On the other hand, it is necessary that managers, for their own effectiveness, comprehend the civic and regional conditions within which they are working, and for their own happiness that they commit themselves to the community in which they live.

6. *The response of labour*

On the labour side there can be little doubt that Glasgow and the west of Scotland have acquired a bad reputation in industrial relations, which compounds the difficulties of the region. Though conflicts between management and men have perhaps been amplified beyond their true dimensions by the emotive label of Red Clyde, and by the media, they are nevertheless a reality, of which the rest of Britain is very conscious. Such a situation and such a reputation are, indeed, what might be expected from an area with such an economic base (containing as it did a higher proportion than the national average of strife-prone industries).

In terms of efficiency wages too, the position in West Central Scotland has been adverse – that is to say, labour costs have been high relative to the value of output, seen in United Kingdom terms. This is a highly complex matter, with many circumstances at work, including the regional industrial structure, the amount and kind of capital, the quality of management, etc. But there is also the possibility that part of the fault has lain with the restrictive practices of labour. The Regional Employment Premium has had some effect in offsetting this adverse labour cost.

With labour, as with management, there have been few studies of an objective kind available to the public. Understandably the unions have not been anxious to become objects of scrutiny by outsiders; moreover they regard themselves as being in continuous tension and frequent conflict with management, so that for them, as with management, secrecy seems essential on tactical grounds. The matter is so sensitive that even government officials are cautious in releasing data on labour relations. Moreover, perhaps by the accidents of survival, though the University of Glasgow and the Glasgow City District Archives have acquired business records on a scale which makes the region one of the best documented in Europe in this sense, it has proved very difficult to acquire parallel material on the labour side, although a beginning has been made.

But it is possible, as in the case of management, to discern certain elements of the picture in a general way. There are responses on the part of labour that are largely traditional and culture-based, derived from past experience and memories and interpretations of it. The most notable of

these is a sense of solidarity, of loyalty to workmates and to class. This can
be augmented by sanctions of a compelling kind. With this goes a strict
insistence on manning and demarcation rules, a challenging of managerial
powers of discipline and a keen eye for victimisation. The fact that most
Clydeside workers live in Corporation houses, or rent-controlled privately
owned ones, rather than owning their house and meeting a mortgage, may
have made striking easier. In contrast to the situation before 1914, the
Clydeside labour force since 1945 has been in a very powerful position, at
least in the short run, tactical sense. This solidarity has meant that the
outlook of the labour force on the objectives it seeks is of great importance.

An American scholar who spent a year in Glasgow early in the 1960s
studying labour and management, observed that 'in regions where the
class conflict is sharpest, as in the west of Scotland, there often seems to be
far more interest in the proportion between the wage level and profits than
in absolute wages. A policy of rising wages which was accompanied by
more rapidly rising profits would be interpreted as a trade union defeat'
(Granick, 1962, p. 185). If the observation was correct, it reflected a
concern with the distribution of the gains of industry between groups,
rather than with living standards as such. But another element has been
present which was similarly a projection of social philosophy, this time in
terms of equity between groups of workers. There has been in the west of
Scotland, in many sectors (including automobiles), a refusal to accept
earnings thought to be inferior to those in other parts of the country; this
has had the result that Glasgow and its region could offer no advantage in
terms of labour costs upon which to build new firms and jobs. The same
demand for 'equality' expressed itself when the UCS workers insisted
upon and got rates equivalent to those of the highest paying (most efficient)
component of the group.

The same American observer accounted for the failure of an incentive
scheme thus: the workers concerned lived in the old slum parts of Glasgow,
by far the worst in Britain. Their rent was negligible: there was little to be
done with additional earnings without stepping beyond the community's
accepted expenditure pattern: such social and residential mobility might
even raise the dreaded question of 'Who does he think he is?' This attitude
was especially strong among the older workers. Generalised, workers'
attitudes toward additional income were related to the long-run aspira-

tions of the family: in a culture where these values which require higher incomes for their realisation are at a discount, wage incentives are unlikely to promote a productivity response.

There has been, too, on the workers' side, a mythology of management which often took little account of the situation within which management has had to act. On the other hand, managements have made mistakes, and have sometimes been devious in their dealings with their workers. There is a sufficient tradition, mostly oral, of management guilt, to stiffen the sense of grievance among workers when required.

It is to be expected that the conditions of the west of Scotland would produce a higher proportion than elsewhere of workmen who have become persuaded that the general system of market relations, as amended by the public sector and by government action, is inadequate, or, indeed downright vicious. On such a premise the logical step was to argue that a different mode of government, intended to bring in a new form of society, should be the objective. Such men have inevitably become powerful voices, raised not for amelioration and improvement, but for fundamental change. The Communist Party by the 1970s held many vital union posts on Clydeside. The International Socialist movement has attracted a good many younger people. Those of leftish persuasion tend to exploit the myth of Red Clyde because it seems to fit their philosophy, seeking to reconstruct historical incidents involving radical action. The UCS work-in provided a striking example of 'the battle for the minds and loyalties of the men among various groups on the left' (Hay and McLauchlan, 1974, p. 27).

Somehow, in at least some sectors of Clydeside industry, there has grown up the idea that it is right to hate the boss, and through him the firm. This attitude in its advanced form seems to be of fairly recent origin and is probably related to the changes that have taken place in the nature of the tasks to be done and the consequent pattern of skills and rewards. It may also have some connection with the rejection of the old paternalism with its accompanying discipline; paradoxically perhaps, it is possible that as the older controls exercised by management have weakened, the old love–hate relationship has lost its love element. Ideology too may have played some part in the development of the anti-boss attitude, though in a somewhat hazy way. The adoption of an attitude of enmity toward the boss has been greatly reinforced by the notion of solidarity, accompanied by powerful sanctions against non-conformists.

A kind of Greek tragedy has resulted. Somehow workers in some sectors have found themselves destroying their firm, fully aware of what they were doing, yet unable to stop. They found themselves answering strike calls when they knew the issue to be of insufficient importance, in the full awareness that in a competitive situation, as in shipbuilding, the result could only be ruin for all concerned. This left only two further stages in the sequence: a demand for subsidy, followed by one for nationalisation.

7. *Investment in Clydeside: incomer firms; external control*

In the circumstances that have obtained it is hardly surprising that it has been difficult to make a new industrial beginning on Clydeside. With so many other regions of Britain eagerly seeking the newer industries, often more free of difficulties inherited from the past, publicising themselves and offering incentives, the adverse image of the West of Scotland has been a severe handicap, and one which in the nature of things seems to be self-confirming rather than self-curing. The nature of Clydeside skills, and its general heavy engineering commitment, was a sufficient disadvantage: to this has been added, by a kind of inevitability, a bad reputation. The West of Scotland has been like a recalcitrant boy subjected to a discipline that further aggravates his condition, closing the circle of negative response. In this situation, the incentive for British capital to embark upon new investment in the West of Scotland was much reduced, giving a further turn to the screw. One of the most disturbing aspects of the picture has been that whereas in the post-war years down to the 1950s, Clydeside received the lion's share of all new economic activity coming to Scotland, this trend was reversed in the 1960s, with Clydeside losing out to the rest of Scotland. To management and labour difficulties there was added a relative failure to invest.

There are three general ways in which capital is attracted to a region. It may come spontaneously in response to projects generated in that region, and offering good returns to outside capital, as indeed occurred in Glasgow in the nineteenth century. This kind of attraction could hardly operate on any scale in the West of Scotland since 1945, for it was difficult to generate such initiatives and few such were forthcoming. Secondly, the government, by various techniques, may subsidise investment in the region, thus creating (through a charge on the tax revenues of the country as a whole) conditions that will overcome the inherent deterrents. This policy has been pursued with some vigour. But its capacity to attract British capital to the West of Scotland has been limited.

This left the third possibility, namely that of enterprises solidly based outwith Scotland, and looking for areas of expansion, like Chrysler, Caterpillar, Euclid or Marathon. Such concerns, by availing themselves of the government aid on offer, could sometimes with profit set up branches in disadvantaged areas. The result on Clydeside was that a high proportion of the newer enterprises that entered the region, relatively modest though they were in aggregate, was foreign owned and controlled. Of the wage earners in factories established in Britain by American firms between 1940 and 1953, 40 per cent are employed in Scotland; this trend seems to have continued since. Such a pattern commits the receiving region to the broader strategy of multi-national businesses, which by their nature compare the relative returns to investment in various countries and act accordingly. It was perhaps something of a paradox that the Communist-led work-in brought such a firm into the very heart of Clydeside pride, the old John Brown yard.

The result of the influx of firms has been the creation of a dual economy in West Central Scotland, with an indigenous element and an incoming one. There has been some tendency for workers to resent externally controlled firms because they are sometimes less easily affected by local trade union opinion and action. But the incoming multi-nationals have acted as the principal innovating force in West Central Scotland, being the means of transmission from international business to the region of new techniques. Unfortunately it would appear that local firms have not been able to respond as creatively as they might have done to the challenge and the needs of the multis; such linkages as have occurred have tended to be among the multis themselves. Japanese and German firms have been hesitant about entering Scotland because they fear they may not be able to handle the kind of labour situation that is likely to arise. Their managerial psychology is not attuned to conflict, but rather to consensus: the workers with whom they deal at home have a primary loyalty to the enterprise, and only a secondary one to their unions.

8. *The syndrome of decline*

Having considered the elements of the regional economy it is possible to construct a generalised syndrome of industrial decline for Glasgow and the West of Scotland, especially after 1960, which is in many ways the obverse of that of the expansion that was characteristic of Glasgow and its region in the years 1875–1914. Just as in the great age of growth the elements acted in a mutually reinforcing way to produce a kind of culmination of confidence and achievement, so in the phase of decline a pattern of mutually sustaining circumstances generated a cumulative and interlocking problem. Glasgow had been passing into this adverse complex when the inflation, incipient since the 1940s, became rampant in the early and mid 1970s, accelerated by the dramatic rise in world oil prices. The city and its region were overtaken, as in the 1930s, by general crisis.

Yet the outcome of Glasgow's problems has not been collapse or anything approaching it: Glasgow is not Calcutta. Indeed the experience of Glaswegians in the years since the war in terms of output, incomes and jobs continues to place them among the world's high-income elite.

As to the future, a return of world prosperity involving a successful purging of inflation and a stabilisation of oil prices at a level that will not damage the world economy, and yet will be high enough to meet the formidable costs of North Sea Oil, would of course benefit Glasgow in common with most British cities. But the degree of such benefit enjoyed will depend on the structure of the regional economy and the motivation present in it among management and labour. If the next phase is to be one of economic disturbance and contraction on a national scale, bringing with it an aggravation of stresses, together with a reduction in disposable funds for the rehabilitation of development areas, the problems will be much more serious.

V. The City Reshaped

1 The new face of Glasgow: planning

HOWEVER stubbornly the economy of Glasgow may have resisted structural change, the performance of the city has been radically different in another sense. Its physical shape – its road system and its major component, namely housing – has been altered since 1945, and largely since 1960, in a truly astonishing way. The matronly war bride who returns on a visit to the city today, or even the emigrant of ten or fifteen years ago, finds that Glasgow has a skyline broken and in many areas dominated by high-rise buildings, with motorways cutting through, over and across older lines of communication, destroying old communal boundaries and providing vistas never seen by earlier generations; the Clyde has been bridged at new levels.

But at the same time the splendid complex of Victorian business buildings in the central business district of the city have been to a great extent preserved, providing a setting in which the tycoons of the past would still be at home. It is an extraordinary picture this – of the core of an inner city where so much remains from the age of confidence, with no significant break in the profile inherited from the Victorians and Edwardians, set in the midst of an outer city in which, though something of the old continues, it is in the interstices of the new, with the greyness of Glasgow's air harmonising with the new greyness of horizontal and vertical features on a new and dramatic scale. The Victorian inner city with Buchanan Street as its spine provides an element of grace and charm encapsulated within a largely revolutionised city. But the inner city is not only a symbol of the achievements of Victorian times, it is also a monument to the lack of pressure on the core of the Central Business District for redevelopment in the 'thirties.

From the early 1950s there was very steady redevelopment by private enterprise in the CBD, in India Street, Waterloo Street, Wellington Street and West Nile Street, reflecting the pressure on available office space. There were arguments in the Corporation from time to time as to whether the provision of office space was excessive, representing improper speculative activity, but the view given by the chartered surveyors was that it increased more or less in step with demand.

Glasgow had a considerable office-building boom from 1963, comparable to that of London. But Corporation policy kept plot ratios low (e.g. the permissible height of buildings as related to the extent of building coverage of the site), and encouraged development on the fringe of the Central Business District. From 1963 the Offices, Shops and Railway Premises Act, by raising the standard of facilities, made a good deal of Glasgow accommodation obsolescent and so increased the pressure for redevelopment on older sites, thus causing Victorian and Edwardian office blocks outside the core of the Central Business District to disappear.

The Central Business District is a place where the initiatives of the private sector predominate, chiefly in the form of shops and offices. The principal means of control is the plot ratio, together with the building regulations, though the rating system (especially the level of rates) has an important impact. The problem for the city is, how to determine these factors so as to cause business firms to produce a CBD that is vigorous and prosperous, and so best able to contribute to civic revenue through the rates.

Housing in Glasgow continued down to the 1960s to reflect the inheritance of the past. The classic four-storey tenement of the nineteenth century, 60 feet high, with a doorless passage from the street and common, uncarpeted stairs, still dominated the city: indeed in 1965 some 85 per cent of all dwellings were in tenements, many black with soot and far advanced in decay. But ownership had greatly changed since 1914: private landlords in 1965 owned 38 per cent of houses, owners occupied their own premises to the extent of 19 per cent, and the Corporation was the landlord of no less than 43 per cent of the housing stock (Cullingworth, 1965).

One result of this pattern has been that effectively the people of Glasgow had almost no stake in house ownership, the greatest single hedge against inflation for most families elsewhere in Britain. This has also added to

---

7. *The Glasgow Exhibition: from the Dome* 1901 Etching
A temporary architectural fantasy overlooking the waterslide and gondolas on the Kelvin.

labour immobility in the geographical sense. At the same time the policy has meant that private building in the city has been negligible; anyone wanting to own a house, has in effect, been obliged to move out of Glasgow. The Corporation's insistence on retaining virtually all sites for subsidised housing has driven private builders outside the city boundaries. There is too the fact that under rent restriction by the state the incentive for land-lords to maintain their 38 per cent of the housing stock as at 1965 has been much diminished, posing a serious threat to the older properties. The element of subsidy to Corporation housing, on the other hand, has been great, placing strain on the finances of the city. The loan debt of the Corporation when it ceased existence in 1975 was £523·8 m. of which £331·4 m. was housing debt. The consequential heavy taxation of com-mercial premises has acted as a deterrent to business and hence employ-ment. High rates may have further encouraged higher income groups to live outside the city to escape this burden, thus reducing taxable capacity, though there is no evidential basis for this. Even the low rents for council houses were partly offset by high rates.

Given the Glasgow problem of an inferior housing stock inherited from the past, together with an economy that has been unable to regenerate itself on a sufficient scale, both present in a context of political democracy, the housing response assumes an air of inevitability.

The remaking of the face of Glasgow since 1945 has provided an intriguing study in how things happen and how things get done. It is a story that begins with a conflict between two views of the proper course of the city's development, held at two different levels of government, the central and the local. The shape of Glasgow was not, therefore, the result of lack of consideration. Indeed there has been since 1945 a more or less continuous debate over the correct development policy for the city. Not one, but two authorities had to be convinced: the Corporation of the city and the Scottish Office. But both had to think in terms of land-shortage.

These matters are perhaps best seen as they evolved over time. During

---

8. *Glasgow Shops* 1899 Etching and Drypoint
College Street on a Saturday night. The shops, with their quarter-bows, are in the ground floors of the tenements. The guttering from the roof discharges in the close-mouth; the street is full of children, many wearing smocks.

F

the war, in 1943, the then Secretary of State for Scotland, Thomas Johnston, convened a committee of all local authorities in the region, which set up a full-time technical sub-committee under Sir Patrick Abercrombie: it produced in 1946 the Clyde Valley Plan. Among the great concerns of the Plan were the congestion of Glasgow and the population saturation of the Clyde Valley. The Report urged that 'in the interests of the City and the region as a whole' there should be a 'planned decentralisation of both population and industry'.

Another great worry of the Report was the tendency for the cities of the region, in spite of geographical and other constraints, to sprawl so that towns straggled into one another. The Plan recommended a green belt which would envelop the region, defining its civic components by pro-viding corridors between them, and so setting limits to their spatial growth. More positively, the green belt would preserve amenity, together with agricultural land. Though the county elements of the green belt were not designated until the mid-'sixties, the appropriate land was kept more or less inviolate until that time.

This green belt doctrine had several implications for Glasgow: in particular the Plan envisaged taking up land within the boundaries of the city. From this there followed a compelling logic. With land for building thus denied, and with congestion already so great in Glasgow, there would have to be a movement of people out of the city. To assist in this it was proposed that four new towns should be built within the green belt, thus making possible a large-scale removal of population from high-density Glasgow to communities planned de novo.

The Scottish Office, representing, of course, the central government, embraced the Abercrombie recommendations. A substantial proportion of Glasgow's population, it believed, should be decanted by means of new towns and 'overspill' agreements with other towns. In taking this view the Scottish Office was following the policy proposed in the Report of the Royal Commission on the Distribution of the Industrial Population, 1940 (the Barlow Report). The Corporation of Glasgow, basing itself on an alternative plan produced by the City Engineer, Robert Bruce, disagreed with the proposal that the city be slimmed in this way, and with emphasis. It argued that if the suggested encroachments of the green belt upon the city were abandoned, rehousing could be carried out within the old boundaries. The Scottish Office was arguing from the currently approved tenets of the planning profession; the Corporation was fighting to maintain the city at more or less its existing size.

In 1947, when the battle between the Secretary of State and the Corporation was at its height, East Kilbride was designated under the New Towns Act of 1946. Though it was not a Glasgow-sponsored new town, being conceived by the Scottish Office as a growth and communal project in its own right, it stood, of course, in relation to Glasgow as a new and rival source of jobs and houses. The Corporation was prevented by the Secretary of State from building on a large section of the land it had purchased at Castlemilk because he was designating East Kilbride.

The Corporation of Glasgow, under strong public pressure, had to act positively to meet the desperate post-war need for housing. Councillors were profoundly conscious of the pressure of the house waiting list, variously estimated in the early 1950s as 80–90,000 families. The Corporation responded by planning and building large housing estates around the perimeter of the city, on green-field sites, using densities a good deal higher than had previously been thought appropriate. Some of the early schemes still contained a significant proportion of cottages, but for the most part the trend was towards rows of three and four-storey walk-up flats. In this way Drumchapel, Easterhouse, Castlemilk, Pollok and Priesthill, each with populations of 25–30,000 came into being. They were, in effect, largely working class dormitory suburbs. These peripheral estates absorbed about 10 per cent of Glasgow's population. So great was the housing emergency that there was minimal provision of facilities and amenities. This seems, however, to have been a failure not at the planning, but at the implementation stage; the plans produced were carefully balanced, providing for the facilities required.

It was when building was imminent that the difficulties became clear. These came under two principal heads. One set had to do with the organisational and legal structure under which the Corporation worked. Neither of these had been thought out and adapted to the task. The Corporation had its Housing Committee and its direct housing agency, plus the necessary powers to build houses. But the agency had very seldom built anything but houses, and the Corporation had no organisation or powers to build shops, picture houses or other facilities to be leased to private enterprise. The position of the Planning Committee was anomalous: it was only in the early 1960s that it was able to acquire its own powers to buy land and lease it, instead of having to act cumbrously through the Housing or Finance Committee. The Planning Committee did not execute, but merely provided the framework with which the executive committees could build: the education authority putting up schools, the Housing Committee building the homes and the highways authority providing the roads and footpaths. This meant that there had to be continuous pressure from the Planning Committee, involving interference in the work of a whole range of other committees.

Secondly, private enterprise was dubious about participation in the schemes, for there was a feeling that the population of an estate would be insufficient to make such facilities viable: each such potential provider had his own criteria. Moreover there was the Corporation's resolution dating from 1890 that public houses should not be provided on Corporation property: this took the heart out of social provision, making it harder to constitute township centres. The problem thus took the form for the Corporation of providing a 'scheme' of houses and planned centres, and then trying to interest the providers of facilities in the private sector to respond, without pubs. Though there was eventually some success in this aspect, as with the Easterhouse township centre, there was no doubt a long period of serious default in which there were no pubs, no picture houses, no libraries, no social centres – there was nothing upon which a community could be based.

Such peripheral housing schemes were thus a kind of parody of the traditional tenement life of Glasgow: they consisted of tenements indeed, but they were far removed from the urban context in which that mode of life had developed, and incapable of generating their own community life. In spite of the literature of planning, already vast, and containing so many hard-learned lessons, these new units were not only devoid of facilities themselves, but were miles from the traditional centre of Glasgow life.

It is easy, of course, to criticise in retrospect what was done in the schemes, but it is important to remember the conditions and atmosphere of the time, together with the inherent difficulties that are always present, in creating, from scratch, and on a large scale, living communities, working under severe cost restraints. Councillors were under enormous pressure from desperate people who would brush aside warnings about the probable lack of facilities, eagerly saying 'it doesnae matter – it's the house we want'. The monthly postcard which showed the councillors the progress of house building was at this time the major criterion for success for the Corporation. Councillors were painfully conscious of the fact that any conceivable programme of new building fell very short of the demand which existed within the city.

Nevertheless, the results have been such as to provide a standing reminder that the provision of housing units is not enough, and that, unless the conditions of true community life are possible within the physical framework provided, there will follow high costs both in money and in social terms. Within the new context of the peripheral estates there soon reappeared social problems well known in the old centre of Glasgow and in Blackhill, including a variant of 'gang' conflict. The spread of television perhaps helped to nullify some of the alienation.

The 1890 resolution that excluded pubs from Corporation property played a rôle of great interest. How was it that a city in which drinking was basic to the culture pattern could bind itself in this way? Did it reflect a middle-class control of Glasgow working-class drinking habits; was it a relic of the Victorian non-conformist conscience, or of the powerful temperance movement of earlier times, or was it a kind of unreasoned reflection of a fear of a hard-drinking tradition? The matter was raised from time to time in the Corporation, but the necessary majority for revocation could not be found: the churches rose in their wrath, tenants' associations (with a high component of women) objected, saying 'We have gone out into the good clean air of the periphery of the city and we don't want pubs here'; there were representations from trade union branches and Labour Party branches. It was not until 1969 that abolition finally came.

Meanwhile in the 1950s the Scottish Office had lost some of its earlier enthusiasm for the regional plan of new towns and overspill (though it showed no signs of modifying its green belt policy). Glasgow Corporation, for its part, also altered its view. By this time a group on the Council were able to persuade their colleagues that such was the physical smallness of the city that it could not keep its population at anything like the densities that had by this time come to be thought appropriate: it would have to adopt an overspill policy on a large scale. This meant accepting a contracting Glasgow. But it was believed that the city could remain a lively, vital place with, say three-quarters of a million population, as in the case of Liverpool, or even less, down to perhaps half a million. Though the danger that the city might denude itself of its more skilled and talented people was raised,

most councillors felt that with a remaining population of three quarters of
a million or less there would still be a lot of bright people and that the
city would not simply be left with a residue. Some councillors still
hankered after the days of the second city of the empire, but most accepted
the logic of reduced densities leading to overspill.

The problem of slums and dereliction in the central parts of the city
urgently demanded attention. The Corporation decided that it must
undertake a major operation on the inner parts of the city. It adopted a
policy of Comprehensive Development, starting with the eastern half of
the notorious Gorbals – Hutchesontown. This policy was approved by
the Secretary of State for Scotland in 1957. The intention was to break up
the old hardcore areas of bad housing, to bring in sunlight and fresh air,
to create space and amenities, to reduce abnormally high infant mortality
rates – in short finally to liquidate the bad inheritance of the nineteenth
century. Such a policy would also help to decongest city centre traffic,
while permitting some extension of Central Business District activities
into Anderston and Cowcaddens. Between 1957 and 1960 Glasgow produced plans for one of the most ambitious slum clearance schemes in
Europe, culminating in the 1960 Development Plan.

The Comprehensive Development Areas were to contain much lower
densities: they were to be reduced from 450 (the average over 29 Redevelopment Areas) to 160 persons per acre (though the Scottish Office
would have preferred an even lower figure), so that 60 per cent of their
population would have to go elsewhere. In some parts the situation was
very much worse, with densities reaching as high as 700 per acre. Such a
programme represented a triumph for the ideas of the 1940 Barlow Report.
But such a reduction of density, of course, added yet further to the land
shortage within the city.

There was a considerable battle in the Corporation over densities,
involving politicians and planners. How was an optimal figure to be
arrived at? Some advisory planners tried to persuade the Corporation that
a higher density than 160 per acre could be made acceptable with modern
buildings, citing American experience. But the Labour Group in the
Council, and the Planning and Housing Committees held to the lower
figure. They had seen so much of overcrowding in Glasgow, and were so
conscious of the past in this respect, that they opted for this enormous
reduction. In some non-redevelopment areas they accepted higher

densities; for example, the Red Road scheme, in a very isolated area, was given densities up to 200 persons per acre.

A second new town, Cumbernauld, had been designated in 1956, and promised some relief. Unlike East Kilbride, it was specifically designated for Glasgow overspill. Under what became known as the 'Cumbernauld conditions' Glasgow was to pay a subsidy of £14 per house per annum for ten years for each family it nominated to the new town. But the Treasury was unwilling to authorise further new towns, largely because the cost had turned out to be much higher than the early optimists had thought.

It was at this point that the proposal for large-scale decanting of population from inner Glasgow contained in the Abercrombie/Clyde Valley Report of 1946 became a live issue. After much discussion the Corporation decided upon a general overspill policy. It would seek to operate a voluntary scheme whereby both people and firms would leave Glasgow and locate themselves elsewhere. The policy was one of population moving out of Glasgow (sponsored by the Corporation) to development areas where industrial employment would be provided by government movement of industry into such areas (using regional incentives). In this sense the Corporation was not directly involved in the attempt to relocate industry in Scotland. Moreover, the movement of industry out of Glasgow was a voluntary matter for firms, depending upon their own judgment of their needs, some firms finding it beneficial to move, and others not. The Corporation did, however, undertake to buy the land and buildings of firms that wanted to overspill under the scheme, and did buy out a number of such firms. Industrial movement was seen mainly as coming from England or America into Scotland. The policy for economic regeneration in Scotland thus consisted of Glasgow overspill of population, with some loss of Glasgow firms, accompanied by an influx into Scotland under government aegis of new firms.

The estimate made in 1960 by the Corporation was that about 200,000 people would have to move from Glasgow by 1980, with the probability of more thereafter, though this was later challenged as an underestimate. The setting of such a figure illustrates the enormous difficulty of arriving at the optimal size for any city. The Corporation entered into agreements with various other local authorities in Scotland to receive the decanted people, building houses for them under the Housing and Town Development Act (Scotland) 1957.

From 1960, then, the policy was that the City would totally rebuild the slum areas, and assist in the dispersal of a significant proportion of its industry and population elsewhere. This was exactly the time at which the faltering of the economy of Glasgow and its region began to become serious, with the heavy industries in deep trouble. But the national economy too was in difficulty. The strengthening of government policy, however, to help the less prosperous regions by controlling industrial development in the more prosperous helped to some extent the Glasgow plans. Also the Scottish Office had developed more confidence in new towns: Livingston, between Edinburgh and Glasgow in the eastern part of Scotland's central belt, was designated in 1962, and Irvine in Ayrshire in 1966. Both came under the 'Cumbernauld conditions'.

The state of the housing stock in Glasgow around 1960 was roughly as follows. The total was around 330,000 units. These divided as to some 215,000 built before 1919, and 115,000 thereafter. The 29 redevelopment areas contained some 110,000 units, one-third of the overall total. Finally, some 97,000 houses were such as not to require attention until after 1980.

Between 1961 and 1975 the overall population of Glasgow fell from 1,055,017 to 825,668, a reduction of more than one-fifth. This was a striking outcome. But in spite of government policy, new firms did not come to Scotland on the scale hoped for, to create new industries and employment in the overspill areas. As to the Glasgow firms it was planned should migrate, between 1957 and 1968 only 6·5 per cent left the city: the dominant tendency was for those firms displaced in the Comprehensive Development Areas to go out of business, or to relocate themselves in the outer parts of Glasgow, or close to the city. Indeed, by 1965 it was accepted that the policy had been only partially successful. Out of the reconsideration thus inspired came the West Central Scotland Plan of 1974.

The relatively limited success of the overspill policy was the result of many factors. The assumption made that firms would move from the redeveloped areas of Glasgow to the reception areas was not sufficiently borne out: the extrusion of firms was one thing, their relocation in the areas desired was another. The new towns drained skills from Glasgow, leaving a residue of unskilled and semi-skilled: whereas Glasgow in 1966 had 2·9 skilled men to each unskilled, the figure for East Kilbride was 14·6. Something of a clash of interests has thus arisen between the New Towns and Glasgow: the New Towns have been favoured, attracting a big effort in terms of investment for the benefit of a relatively small element of the total population, whereas the outer city of Glasgow has been left with inferior facilities. The workers displaced from Glasgow were equally the subject of over-optimistic assumptions: many were understandably reluctant to move to overspill areas, involving a change of place and possibly of job. Many, too, were in the outcome losers, for though they might benefit from living in new areas through housing subsidies and other advantages, they were also involved in losses in so far as their jobs were not relocated as was their housing, thus creating dislocation costs in the form of fares and travelling time.

A new national body was brought into existence in 1964, largely on a non-party basis. This was the Housing Corporation, intended to supply possibilities additional to municipal housing or outright private ownership, in the form of co-ownership and fair rent schemes (under which subsidy of the rents in the private sector might arrest deterioration of the privately-owned housing stock). The Glasgow office of the Housing Corporation has concerned itself largely with the rehabilitation and improvement of existing houses rather than the building of new ones, and has been instrumental in setting up a number of community-based housing associations in older parts of the city – Govan, South Dennistoun and Govanhill. These activities have provided, in a sense, an alternative to municipal ownership.

Glasgow is the centre of a new venture, the Planning Exchange, begun in 1972. Its object was to bring together the participants in planning – the practising professional, the academic and the politician. Originally financed by the national government and the Ford Foundation, it was later supported by the Scottish Development Department and the Scottish Local Authorities. The city thus contained a forum and a research unit of a unique kind.

2. High-rise flats

In spite of the Comprehensive Development Areas and the overspill policy, the problem of land scarcity within the city remained. It is worth noting in comparative terms that Edinburgh, with about one-half of Glasgow's population in 1960 had a superficial area of 36,000 acres as against Glasgow's 40,000; the corresponding Birmingham figure for a population roughly that of Glasgow's was 60,000 acres.

There was one further possibility for the Corporation of Glasgow – namely the building of multi-storey flats. This seemed an attractive course for other reasons. There had been striking developments in systems building which seemed to hold great potential; moreover high-rise flats, built by large consortia, could add to the number of housing units much more quickly than could any other programme. Of course, subsidy would be required, as with any Glasgow housing programme. Accordingly the policy of going out (overspill) was accompanied by going up (multi-storey flats).

To move in this direction was a revolutionary step: it meant altering the nature of urban living for many people to something not previously known in Glasgow. The old tenement life was no true antecedent to life in high-rise flats: the tenements had been on the human scale, easy to walk into and about, capable of engendering real communities. The necessity of installing a lift meant that there was a jump from four to at least ten storeys, representing a new way of life. Though some planners expressed misgiving, the policy was carried through. For, once again, near emergency conditions prevailed; there were intense social and political pressures. The planners seemed to be caught between the natural conditions of the Clyde Valley, the political boundary of the City of Glasgow, the inheritance of the past in terms of density and incomes, and rising expectations. From the late 1950s they were committed to the new high-rise formula for living.

The speed at which the skyline of Glasgow was transformed was remarkable: the major change took place within ten years after 1960. By 1968 there were six times as many multi-storey housing units being built to every low-rise; by 1969 163 blocks had been brought into occupancy. By that year the Corporation's Housing Management Department had 15,000 high-rise units on its books alongside 121,500 low rise homes. The new mode of life reached its extreme in Red Road, where a complex of slab blocks of 31 storeys comprised an estate composed almost wholly of high flats, 300 feet high, as against the 60 feet of the traditional tenements. At one stage 41 storeys were proposed, but after a battle ten were knocked off.

The high-rise flats brought real gains. Many tenants appreciated the flats themselves, with their modern facilities so marvellously different from the conditions from which they had come; the houses were in this sense successful. But with use, many disadvantages began to appear. Older people tended to be isolated, and families with young children found access to the world outside the flat difficult. You shut your door, and you were on your own. There was too, the problem of maintenance, especially of the indispensable lifts, of the stairs, the communal areas and of the environs of the flats which could so easily deteriorate. Moreover, the money cost of such flats, in spite of expectations, proved very high. It would seem, too, that the economies of space upon which so much thinking was based have been, at least in part, illusory. The policy of building high flats, therefore, like that of overspill, reached the limits imposed by experience.

But there remained the continuous task of reducing the social disadvantages and creating real communities. It may be that the full importance of tenant selection was not realised; that not enough work was done on the considerations that ought to have applied when bringing families of varying social structures together in high-rise blocks. If so, there is a potential for improvement here. Tenant communal initiative too has varied a good deal: in some blocks the tenants' meeting room has been very little used, whereas in others the tenants have introduced carpets, seating, plants and the like, creating a communal facility.

3. The new road system

But already yet another challenge had been added to those of density and housing. A new claimant upon Glasgow's inadequate supply of land was asserting itself. This was the road system. The demolitions in the Central Development Area had created what appeared to be a prime opportunity for the remaking of Glasgow's internal communications. The Bruce Plan of 1945 and the Clyde Valley Plan of 1946 had taken some account of the problem as it had existed in the mid-'forties; the Highway Plan of Scott, Wilson, Kirkpatrick and Partners was presented in 1965. It urged that the city be provided with a new system of three concentric roads and ten major radial ones. The adoption of such a programme was a decision on the same scale as that involved in opting for multi-storey flats. In 1975 it was on schedule: the Clyde Tunnel, the Kingston Bridge, the Clydeside Expressway and half of the Inner Ring Road existed, and the

West–east M8 was well on the way to completion. Some 7,000 houses were pulled down to make room for the new road system. Driving along the Glasgow motorways there is a strange sensation of passing through the ghosts of tenements where life in all its intimacy and complexity has been lived. But by the time they were pulled down it was better that they should go, being much decayed: the greater part of the inner ring was deliberately planned to go through housing that would have in any event to be removed.

The opponents of the road scheme were articulate and condemnatory. They argued that the scheme was entirely misconceived, especially on the part of a Labour Council. It had meant, it was said, paying minimal attention to the transport needs of those with modest or low incomes and had placed greatest emphasis on allowing free movement to the automobile in a city in which the level of car ownership was less than one-half that of Britain as a whole; at the same time it ruptured the classic pattern of Glasgow's urban life in which its people have always lived.

The counter-arguments were that it was essential to create a new Glasgow, to clear much of the old living and manufacturing areas, and, in the opportunity thus brought about, to construct a system of roads that would provide quick and convenient movement into, out of, around and within the city. Such a programme was greatly aided by government capital grants of 75 per cent. These made road building highly attractive; indeed a heavy bias in this direction was induced by the central government, for what councillor could vote against a provision costing only 25 per cent? But road building had a strong appeal on its own account. The concept of urban renewal, so powerful in the 1960s, could, it was hoped, be implemented with the road system as a central element. There was, too, the urge to alter the old image of the city held elsewhere by business men and others, replacing it with a sense of growth and responsiveness.

All five elements (the overspill/green belt policy, new towns, Comprehensive Development Areas, high flats and a motorway system), had, by 1975, encountered limitations. Partly this was because of the exhaustion of their potential or disillusionment with their product, and partly it was because the general state of the economy imposed a pause. But Glasgow had been irreversibly changed by the destruction or debilitation of so many of its component village communities: the old Crosses on which life and communications had focussed were now largely meaningless.

4. Allocation and authority

Whereas in 1965 43 per cent of Glasgow's housing stock was under public ownership, the figure in 1971 was 54·2 per cent. By 1975 it stood at just over 57 per cent, that is, some 158,000 houses out of 275,000. The increase was largely at the expense of the privately rented sector, where, under rent restriction, deterioration and sometimes abandonment had occurred. Some wards are almost totally owned by the Corporation, for example, Provan, Yoker, Knightswood, Pollokshaws and Ruchill. This vast collection of housing units is administered by the Housing Management Department with its House Letting Department at Clive House.

The Housing Management Department became a kind of local leviathan – a massive landlord with a bureaucratic organisation to which has been entrusted much of the life of the city. The applicants for houses far exceeded the available accommodation over any given period – in 1972 no less than 15,863 families on the waiting list were classified as homeless, though such lists are not always a safe guide. The disposable housing stock was characterised by a wide range of acceptability – as to size of house, form, location and level of rents and rates, with Group 8 containing the least desired. The claims of house-seekers were equally diverse, but divergent from the supply. The behaviour of tenants was also highly various – some being conscientious and others destructive.

Of all this the Corporation, through the Housing Management Department, had become the arbiter. A group of administrators had been given the task of housing allocation, with all the attendant social implications. The situation had evolved so far away from market criteria that others had to be found. Ultimately there was no escape from some sort of points system based upon need, combined with a grading of tenants based upon behaviour intended to determine their appropriateness for one neighbourhood or another. In addition applicants were offered a number of choices of house. The life of a family could be dominated by the great landmark of the move to a better house; most families accordingly accepted the system as a datum, setting about to meet its requirements. A minority of families would or could not conform.

The Housing Management Department has always been anxious to find occupants for the less attractive parts of its housing stock, to shorten as far as possible periods of emptiness (with accompanying vandalism), and to minimise anti-social behaviour and default on rents. At the same time it had always to fight against its own bureaucratic insensitivity, born of a virtually impossible task. As one councillor put it: 'It is never easy to deal with the public, especially when the public think you have a facility that they want, and they feel their need to be desperate.' The Housing Department was, of course, answerable to the Corporation, and through it to the electorate.

But it proved very difficult for the system to be made subject to democratic control in its day-to-day operations. These have involved rehousing as many as 9,000 people in Glasgow every year. Perhaps insufficient thought was given to the House Letting Department, for in spite of the fact that the Corporation's public image largely depended upon it, it was one of the least well-equipped Departments. There was, too, the question of housing philosophy: the task was seen as one of the management of housing rather than in terms of helping people. Perhaps housing managers and janitors in multi-storey flats should act not only as factors and caretakers concerned with the city's property, but also to some degree as social workers interested in the people, providing a focus, a sustained and supportive interest.

Meanwhile, a second leviathan had come into being, namely the Planning Committee and its Department. Its job was to determine the physical shape of the city, including the great reconstruction and housing schemes. As in other cities the bulldozer has been used in Glasgow on working class areas with a minimum of consultation and almost no resistance. Communities have been disrupted and destroyed by decisions taken from above, bringing great changes in the social fabric of working class life. But so great was the scale of the problem of renewal, and so large and complex the nature of the operations involved, requiring the demolition of nearly 100,000 houses, that there was a heavy discount upon consultation of those to be affected, and a good deal of denial of information. Moreover, in the older inner parts of the city working class communities were profoundly infected by apathy and hopelessness.

But the ruthlessness can be exaggerated. The Pollokshaws redevelopment for example was held up for six months while attempts were being made to find accommodation for one last old man who was living in one last old house. Moreover, though the people affected were not asked about particular clearance schemes, the felt need for better housing so that the quality of family life could be improved, was very powerful and highly vocal.

It has been suggested that working class communities should no longer be treated as though passive and impotent, but that there should be a development of community control over neighbourhoods with local participation in services and institutions. Much of the major surgery on the city has now been carried out, though there are still one or two areas where the bulldozer rather than the improving team is indicated. It may be that it will be possible to move away from imposed solutions to participatory ones, perhaps through community councils.

5. The planning achievement

In spite of much continued suffering, and of resentments against planners and bureaucrats, a major improvement in Glasgow life was achieved between 1945 and 1975. The desperate densities of the past had vanished and the crowded core of the city inherited from the nineteenth century had been remade. No less than 100,000 municipal houses had been built since the war, and at the same time the city had decanted some 200,000 people, about one-fifth of its total. The percentage of households with exclusive use of hot and cold water, a fixed bath and an inside WC, though lower than the steadily rising national average, improved between 1961 and 1971 from 58·9 per cent to 75·2 per cent. The percentage of the population living at more than 1·5 persons per room fell from 46·9 in 1951 to 26 in 1971.

The infrastructure, too, had been remade, so that traffic congestion has been greatly eased and speed of movement increased. The new road system has a drama and a verve of its own, opening up new panoramas of the city from the Clydeside Expressway and elsewhere, making visible the excitement of an industrial landscape and its setting of encircling hills. Though Glasgow still has its decayed and depressing parts, it has been given a new kind of urban image.

There has certainly been a coercive aspect to the clearing of the ground for both new housing and infrastructure. But it may be that to operate upon the scale required, within the necessary cost and timing limits, some at least of this was unavoidable. Certainly money has not been lacking.

Nor has effort. The rebuilding of Glasgow has not been the outcome of blind brutalism. Much consultation and discussion went into the many aspects of so vast an undertaking; the research base was often elaborate and careful. But it is never enough, partly because many of the questions to be asked do not become apparent until a commitment has been made. There was too, the need, in order that situations be made manageable, to reduce them to over-riding formulae. The three most important of these were the setting of plot ratios for the Central Business District, the establishment of densities for redevelopment areas, and the setting of the overspill figure (and through it the appropriate size of the city as a whole). Politicians and planners are certainly fair targets for public criticism, but their job of urban renewal should be seen in its totality, and over time.

VI. *Culture and Politics*

1. *Identity and image*

AS GLASGOW has been thus changing, how have its denizens regarded themselves, both in their relations with one another and with the world beyond?

Though the east–west and north–south divisions have largely remained, the city has not been so distinct or symmetrical as in the past. Before 1914 there had been two cultures shared within a single city, each with its strong ethos, each largely unknown and inaccessible to the other, each maintaining its geographical separation, except when encountering the other in the shopping and entertainment streets. Much of this altered in the 'fifties and 'sixties. Television was a great agent for bringing the way of life of one social group into the living rooms of another. The private car, in spite of its relatively low incidence in Glasgow, made people more mobile, so that all drivers and passengers shared the same roads, and often the same frustrations and the same destinations. The rebuilding of Glasgow, in revolutionising its shape, caused people to pass through other people's territory to and from work (although motorways have often brought a new isolation from social contact). Alas, under such circumstances vandalism also spread.

But perhaps more important than all of these new conditions, society itself had been changing. By the 'seventies the mandarinism of the great age of Glasgow prosperity has been much diminished: among business men postures of aloofness, inaccessibility and high policy were disappearing. Managements became aware that they must come to terms with their labour forces on the basis of consent rather than paternalism or edict. The disparity of post-tax incomes was now greatly reduced: the General Manager of a Scottish bank before 1914 might receive after tax 40 or 50 times the salary of a clerk; this compared with about 5 times in the 1970s. As a reflection of this the gap in class terms between life-styles was a good deal diminished. But there can be no doubt that as between a working-class family living in a scheme or a high-rise flat, and a middle-class family in

G

the West End or Bearsden or in Newton Mearns, a real gulf persisted.

It may be, indeed, that, in spite of greater mobility and mixing of the classes, and the reduction of the gross gap in incomes, the sense of class difference has heightened. Glasgow has generated a labour force containing one of the highest proportions among British cities of workers with a low level of skills, together with one of the lowest proportions of professional and managerial people, and so is increasingly a working-class city.

Within the working classes there continue to be strong differences and even antipathies. A Marxist sociologist would say of the skilled, higher income element that has moved out of Glasgow to Bishopbriggs, that they have become 'incorporated' into the middle class, accepting values taken to be exclusively characteristic of that class. Schoolboys growing up in the east end of Glasgow in the 'fifties expressed their own view of Bishopbriggs as Spam Valley, a reference to the belief that its inhabitants, burdened with mortgage payments, could afford nothing better than spam sand-wiches.

The middle classes are of course still an important element in Glasgow life. Stanley Baxter with his perceptive television projection of the speech and outlook of Kelvinside has provided a stereotype of middle-class artificiality and pretension that is pretty cruel. Members of the middle class have certainly been critical of trade union behaviour and reciprocal condemnation of management has not been lacking.

The cultural achievement in which Glasgow can take justifiable pride, has been largely a middle-class affair. The restoration of the Theatre Royal to house Scottish Opera is a success unique in Britain. The Scottish National Orchestra has a national reputation in Britain and has begun to create an international one. The Citizens' Theatre ranks high among Britain's repertory companies. The Art Galleries of the city give it a similar national ranking. The same is true of its two Universities and its colleges. Much care and money has been expended in the preservation of notable buildings. In short, the high culture of the city is not inconsiderable. But it is still to a great degree middle class, with minimal working-class participation.

The mass influx of newcomers which had been so striking an aspect of Glasgow life in the years before 1914 had largely dried up by 1945 – there was no great inflow of Highlanders, Irish, Jews or other Europeans. Even immigration from the Commonwealth had relatively little effect upon Glasgow and its region, for high unemployment acted as a buffer against such a movement. By and large, only the better educated Asians had ventured north, together with industrious small business men. There was no great addition to the labour force, though Glasgow's transport department has come to rely upon Pakistanis to a considerable extent. The process of assimilation seems to have gone smoothly, though Bashir Maan, the first elected Pakistani member of the Corporation, has given a warning: 'As newcomers to the country we tolerate many things, but will our kids be prepared to do the same?'

Among the working classes of the west of Scotland there has continued a strong sense of common experience, reflected in the collective memory, in anecdote and in speech. It is linked with a fierce local loyalty. This has remained so in spite of all the physical changes. It is rooted in a common past and in shared realities.

Among the few groups in society who can interpret the social elements of Glasgow to themselves and to one another are its folksingers and its poets. The *Clydeside Litterateurs* of the later nineteenth century showed little real interest in their city, except as a foil for their strong nostalgia for the Scottish countryside, Highland and Lowland; the spirit of Sir Walter Scott was strong upon them still; their urgent feeling for the idyllic and the heroic made them curiously impervious to the real circumstances which dominated their lives. Against this attitude might be placed a remark by Ken Dodd that highlighted the fact that a society is only to be understood by direct contact. Dodd dismissed the romantic and the theorist thus: 'The trouble with Freud is that he never played the Glasgow Empire Saturday night.'

But the 'sixties and 'seventies saw a new race of writers and singers who, though some of them may have complained that university and college courses are a stultifying experience, had a sense of relevance and a wealth of reference never before available. They had acquired, too, ideas from the social sciences and the great social critics. But they started, not by considering the economic and social basis of things in an analytical way, but from observation and feeling.

In Edwin Morgan's poems can be sensed the horror of the nether end of the scale of Glasgow deprivation. He welcomes and yet resents the impact of the demolition men's ball as it breaks up the Glasgow of Joan Eardley's movingly painted urchins. But the reader also shares a sense of excitement at the new motorways and the giant yellow cranes each lifting about and beneath itself the fabric of a tower. Morgan, with Charles Rennie Mackintosh in mind, described how

> . . . the flyovers breed loops of light
> in curves that would have ravished tragic Toshy –
> clean and unpompous, nothing wishy-washy.

On reflection, however, as new problems emerged from this massive manipulation of the city, the excitement that at last something constructive was happening faded and doubt entered. As Edwin Morgan, contemplating the scale and complexity of the problem, has said, 'a great place and its people are not renewed lightly'.

One of the most interesting aspects of the new poetic voice of the west of Scotland is the strong assertion of a working class point of view and of local cultural self-containment. Liz Lochhead, sitting on Midsummer Common in Cambridge, compared the harmonious and genteel aspects of what she saw around her to her home setting of Motherwell – a steel town, with its leaden sky, its endless rain, its football rowdies, its cinema queues, the palais, social clubs, litter and slag heaps. There is a resentment that such an idyllic Cambridge scene diminishes people from another background. Behind this attitude seems to lie a statement of the validity of life spent among working class people in an industrial city.

Ewan MacColl, raised in Lanarkshire, has expressed another reaction in his song 'Dirty Old Town'; that of a man capable of nostalgia, yet yearning for a renewal:

> I met my love by the gasworks croft,
> Kissed my girl by the old canal,
> Dreamed a dream by the factory wall,
> Dirty old town, dirty old town. . . .

Glasgow has produced in the 'seventies two spokesmen from and for its working classes who have been projected by the media on a national scale. They are Jimmy Reid and Billy Connolly.

Jimmy Reid has been highly active politically through the UCS work-in and the Communist Party, and was chosen Rector of Glasgow University in 1971 when its students were in a mildly leftish phase. Highly articulate and deeply sincere, he has appealed for a new moralism and a rejection of the materialist society and the 'rat race' it imposes. Though he can participate in the rude humour of the shipyards, he does not use it in his public appearances. Instead he is serious to the point of dedication, condemning the 'uncaring society' and urging a form of socialism that would promote human brotherhood, but which is imprecise as to mechanics both economic and political. He is a moralist-populist, to whose idealism the academic young have responded. He is a man from among the workers who has been awarded the status almost of prophet, but who has been denied political support by his own people of Clydebank. Jimmy Reid projects the working classes in a highly serious vein, as the source of the nation's wealth and as the repository of its true values.

Billy Connolly, the 'Big Yin' (the Big One) has been a highly successful public entertainer since the *Great Northern Welly Boot Show* in the early 1970s. He is one of the first Scots comics to make a national mark in the age of electronic entertainment. He goes about things quite differently from Jimmy Reid. The working classes are the basis of his performance. There is no attempt to idealise them – the life of the tenements and the brutalism it can produce are the base level from which he works. The old favourites so dear to Lex McLean and other veterans of Glasgow's Pavilion are still there, with their slang variants, the chamber pot (chanty), getting drunk (bevvyed), seduction (pulling the lumber), and so on. But they are given a new directness and amplification: what would have been a mention a decade or so ago is now an elaborate story with sound effects. The leaps Connolly has made in the direction of the explicit are such that his works, by going so far beyond the expected, can be very funny. From the lavatorial he has progressed to religion, bringing it down to the level of fun in a way that can be pretty cruel, and is offensive to those, usually older people, who retain older beliefs.

And yet there is a kind of idealism. Connolly has a loyalty to his 'punters' (supporters) that is important to him. He says that he would not, for example, accept a decoration from the Queen. He thus seems to see himself as in some sense as reflecting and projecting the values of his punters. But what are these values? When he describes a drunken tenement party, is he celebrating a good side of working-class life? Does he see himself as a sweeper-away of cobwebs – destroying Victorian and Knoxian inhibitions, bringing the cleansing breeze of frankness into modern life? Certainly the middle-classes are obnoxious to him: Milngavie and Bearsden are where the hypocritically respectable stay, the bosses who run a petty tyranny in the shipyards and elsewhere. Anarchic protest is a standing theme of Connolly's – he projects his working-class life and that of his peers as one of evading the rules and discipline of a corrupt society, scoffing at those who abide by them. This, projected in songs and stories, with show-business backing, has a strong appeal. But it is impossible to find in it any of the moralism which means so much to Jimmy Reid, much less any hint of an alternative society.

In the past, what teachers have taught in Glasgow schools has often been an implied criticism of the way of life of a considerable proportion of parents: this is true of speech, manners and general outlook on the way life is lived. In the later 'sixties and early 'seventies this to some degree changed, with a good many teachers seeking to identify less with middle class mores, and to find elements of intrinsic value in working class life. The difficulty, of course, is to know what parts of middle class behaviour to retain and what parts of the working class mode of life to adopt, and what synthesis to make of the two. Cultural democratisation of this kind involves the reconciliation of deeply-rooted differences and the overcoming of mutal fears.

In the meantime there is the image held of Glasgow's culture in Britain and in Europe. It is curiously equivocal. There is the feeling that Glasgow can still generate energy, revel in individuality and aggressively assert itself. This provides a legend of vigour and barbarity which may be attractive in a Britain which is seen as subsiding into senility. This view is accompanied by a sense of warmth, of shared hospitality, together with a powerful native wit. But the obverse view is less attractive and economically damaging: it is that of a place where the level of violence is significantly higher than elsewhere and where the labour force is more intractable than most. In short hardly a good place in which to invest.

People do not expect gentle things to come out of Glasgow; there is a feeling that so far north, amid the clang and clamour of heavy industry the veneer of civilisation is perilously thin, scarcely able to contain the elemental urges beneath. Evelyn Waugh reflected this view when he defined Hogmanay as being sick on the pavement in Glasgow. All this, whatever truth it may contain, is secondary. The basic problems have been economic, having to do with the provision of jobs and housing, both to a significant degree inherited from earlier generations.

2. Deprivation, delinquency and disintegration

The social problems of cities come to a focus in terms of those people least well provided for, the residuum in and around whom deprivation centres. Assisting this most disadvantaged part of urban society presents enormous difficulties. The provision of so much new housing in Glasgow (between 1960 and 1974, 53,000 municipal houses and about 2,500 private houses were built) acted in the direction of amelioration. Some 85,000 houses in the city were withdrawn from the housing stock, representing much of the worst of the old. But there was little improvement in the position of Glasgow's poorer elements, compared with the rest of Britain.

It is important, however, not to take too gloomy a view. Standards were continuously rising in Britain as a whole, constituting, in a sense, a receding target. In average per capita terms incomes in the city are now not very different from those of the United Kingdom as a whole. Glasgow certainly has its share of good incomes: the situation is not one of a population that is desperately poor. On the other hand, however, the city does contain a big tail of very poor people, well in excess of the national average.

In terms of deprivation, indeed, the city since 1945 has presented a picture a good deal worse than that suggested by the relative performance of its economy. Though not all authorities are agreed on the statistical techniques employed, the indicators of urban deprivation based upon the 1971 census seem to reveal Clydeside to be by far the most dramatic case in Britain. In one aspect after another Glasgow, it is argued, had the worst provision of any city in the United Kingdom – in overcrowding, in lack of bathroom facilities, in unemployment (especially males), in the low proportion of motor cars. In most of these aspects Glasgow appears to be not simply marginally different from other British cities, but worse to a melancholy degree, much greater than would be suggested by employment or income differentials. Of course some account must be taken of Glasgow's historical differences from other cities, especially the traditionally smaller proportion of family budgets spent on house space. But in spite of all qualifications, the degree of deprivation in the city is striking.

Inferior general living conditions have been reflected in health standards: Glasgow has a worse record than other cities of comparable size in Britain in terms of lung cancer, cancer of the large bowel, and respiratory disease, as well as being a place where a majority of the population have lost their teeth by the age of forty. All this has been accompanied by a high level of alcoholism and morbid aggression.

The impression given by these indicators of living conditions is reinforced by the general appearance of the city, especially certain parts of it, alas all too visible to the incomer and the visitor. Graffiti, litter, vandalised bus shelters, heavy shutters or grilles for shops, all bear witness to the link between deprivation and disintegration. The Scottish Office has been much concerned at the high depreciation rate of Glasgow council houses, especially those of ten to fifteen years old, due to physical damage. The same kind of destruction can be seen in Edinburgh's problem schemes, but they are less dominant in the city as a whole. Glasgow conduct at football matches provides further evidence of tension and declining social discipline: Maurice Lindsay in his *Glasgow Nocturne* gives a picture of youthful gangs which:

> Materialised from the flaked stones of buildings
> dark with neglect and poverty, the pack,
> thick-shouldered, slunk through rows of offices
> squirting anonymous walls with their own lack
>
> of self-identity. Tongs ya bass, Fleet,
> *Fuck the Pope* spurted like blood . . .
>
> violence sneaked out in banded courage,
> bored with hopelessness that has nothing to lose.

This kind of urban problem is present in all cities: the graffiti in a new town like Cumbernauld has reached a level approaching that of Glasgow, not to mention other major British cities like Manchester or Liverpool; so too with football rowdies. As in labour relations, the world has embraced a Glasgow stereotype, often aided by expatriates as they expatiate on their native city. Nevertheless, in comparative terms, the Glasgow situation is as bad as any, if not the worst.

The hard-core slum dwellers of Glasgow before 1914 included many debilitated people, low in energy and initiative: the problem since the 'fifties has centred around youths who, for all the inadequacy of their lives,

were reasonably well-fed, and hence vigorous, able to express their alienation and frustration in violence and vandalism, presenting a threat to
ordered society that the dense dark places of the Victorian and Edwardian
city could not produce. Whereas the worst slums of the nineteenth century
had been places of concentration for immigrants, especially Irish, those
of the nineteen-sixties and 'seventies were of Glaswegians, many of them
hereditary slum dwellers.

It may be that social deprivation is related to the performance of the
regional economy in such a way that a short-fall in adaptation and growth
in commerce and industry has produced a more than proportional adverse
result in social terms, a kind of 'gearing up' effect. Thus a city with an
employment rate of 95 per cent instead of the national average of some
98 per cent may have indicators of deprivation much higher in proportion.
This will be especially the case where, as with Glasgow, there has been
a carry-over of inferior social capital (especially houses) from earlier times.

The phenomenon of deprivation tended to some degree to be officially
minimised from 1945 onward: the Labour Party in Glasgow as elsewhere,
having added so greatly to earlier welfare provisions, tended to play down
the existence of large-scale poverty and of serious gaps in basic physical
equipment for homes, together with omissions in the welfare services. The
dislike of adverse publicity for the city confirmed this attitude. There was,
too, the enormous challenge of the rebuilding of Glasgow, a preoccupation
which naturally took precedence. The problems of the city were so vast
that there might well have been a temptation to obscure them, or at least
to define them in such terms as to make them manageable, under given
assumptions about available resources. This would mean that public
statements of the city's needs would be in terms of feasibility, rather than
of objective measurement. But the appearance of *Born to Fail?*, the outcome of work by the National Children's Bureau in England in 1972/3
revived deprivation as a subject of public concern. Because of lack of basic
studies in Scotland, the further questions of the relationships between
deprivation and social disintegration have hardly been raised.

Extreme deprivation has produced much petty crime, and even more
nuisance behaviour, drunkenness and rows as well as malicious mischief.
But the reaction to the frustrations of deprivation, or to living in an
environment which inhibits the majority of positive drives has been a dual
one. It has produced in some the 'healthy' reaction of delinquency. In

others it has induced neurosis, the curling in upon oneself, producing what
Brennan (1959) called the 'grey scrubbers'.

By the mid-'sixties there were no *criminal* areas left in Glasgow, that is
areas in which criminals were known to reside in sizeable groups, for this
would have meant far too great a vulnerability to the police, with their
cars and radios, able to go anywhere by day or night (Mack, 1964). But
delinquent neighbourhoods had survived and indeed grown, areas which
produced young offenders in exceptionally large numbers, a high proportion
of whom graduated from delinquency to adult criminality. In such
neighbourhoods the values and practices of the wider society are rejected
by the prevailing social tone; dishonesty and minor violence are accepted
as a way of life. Even here, however, the acceptance is passive rather than
active. The worst street in Blackhill (252 houses), produced between 1948
and 1960 20 deliquent offenders per 100 houses of whom 29 per cent
became adult criminals. It is difficult to avoid the conclusion that crime is
in large measure a product of the social structure, the result of people
becoming only too well adjusted to their local community, their sub-
culture. The big trials on Clydeside, especially that of the murderer Peter
Manuel in 1958, threw much light on the regional criminal network as it
then existed.

It is not of course true that all the ills of urban life are to be found among
the most deprived. But a high proportion are, especially if we mean not
only the lack of those physical facilities which are often taken to be its
indicators, but even more important, a situation in which the communal
sub-culture has become hostile to the larger society. It must be a matter of
continuous concern to improve the Glasgow situation in these regards.
In the meantime social workers have often had hopeless case-loads, often
composed of grey scrubbers rather than healthy delinquents.

Such social workers have been placed under enormous strain, posing the
problem of maintaining energy and inspiration among those who are concerned with such problems. It is scarcely surprising that there has been a
conflict in the minds of many social workers (especially perhaps the
younger ones) between the patching-up functions they perform and
political radicalism. But teachers, housing managers, doctors, and indeed
all who have to do with deprived areas share the problem of maintaining
their commitment.

Another aspect concerns the police and the courts: how in the short run, to contain the sub-culture of violence? A much greater solicitude about civil liberties has inhibited police action. Billy Connolly, who grew up in Partick in the 'fifties, describing the change in police behaviour towards boys caught in doubtful situations, remarked: 'It was the end of the kick-in-the-arse era, just before "If I catch you I'm going to tell yer faither".'

And yet, in spite of all, even the worst housing schemes contain many people, indeed a majority, who are good citizens and who regret and resist the deterioration around them. They, and the continually renewed young, are the justification given for costly modernisation and improvement projects which may help to set limits to the decline of local communities by removing some aspects at least of deprivation, so that it may do less damage over successive generations. But, as with the problems of efficiency and productivity in the regional economy, it is not enough to try to purge the symptoms of social failure by pumping in public money; more profound remedies are required, involving a much deeper understanding of outlook and motivation, and of the social processes that produce them.

It may be that some areas are beyond redemption, that it is impossible, for example, to regenerate Blackhill. This leaves the solution of clearance of the site, as partially adopted at Ferguslie Park in Paisley. But this, of course, poses the problem of where the people are to go and their impact when they get there.

The relationship between deprivation and the breakdown of the individual, the family and local society is not, of course, a simple one. Through the nineteenth century and onward there have been families in the poorer areas of Glasgow that have withstood the effects of bad conditions, maintaining their unity and integrity; indeed this may well have happened more often than not. It may have derived from a set of values and sanctions that have been losing their power, or it may have rested upon inner resources that made it possible to live in deprivation without falling into disintegration.

3. *The quality of public management: the Labour Town Council*

The evolution of the economy and society of Glasgow through prosperity and contraction produced, of course, its own characteristic political response. It was by a kind of natural law that the city should go Labour, both in parliamentary and local government terms. Whereas before 1914 the Corporation was seen as a joint-stock company run by the middle classes, since 1933 it has been increasingly a social service run by the Labour Party, centred upon public-sector housing at low rents.

At the parliamentary level, in periods of near-equipoise in the House of Commons, the Scottish Labour vote centred on the west became crucial for Labour governments. This could give the city great leverage. In civic terms the outcome was something pretty close to one-party government, with the Labour Party exercising a self-confirming grip on affairs: this trend, now apparent in many Italian cities, has been present in Glasgow since the later 1930s. Opposition inevitably became discouraged, having little hope of power.

But the politicians were only part of the picture. As the functions of local government grew, so too did the number and standing of professional administrators, together with the planners. These groups each developed its own characteristic professional outlook, which was brought to bear both in advising the politicians and in carrying out policy. The result was an involved interplay between politicians and their public servants, often mediated by priorities and premiums coming from the Scottish Office and the central government.

Many of the planners were incomers to Glasgow and to Scotland, attracted by the challenge of remaking a major city. So far as they as a profession have been concerned, they seem to have taken a positive line until recently, assuming some of the professional omniscience of doctors, confidently advocating formulae generated from within their profession. In more recent years the positiveness has been a good deal modified as the true complexities of the social and economic fabric have become more apparent. It is to be hoped, however, that what might appear to some as arrogance will not be replaced by impotence, for the will to act is essential, even when there is less emphasis on grand design and more on urban management.

The programme for the remaking of Glasgow seems to have been conceived mainly in physical terms, rather than in terms of cost. It is impossible to find out, without great effort, the total investment that has been made by the government in the regeneration of the city, or its component parts.

The Labour councillor, the heir to the tradition of protest, has been caught in the toils of massive but intricate processes of social and physical manipulation. The planner and the administrator, each with his professional responsibility, has carried out those policies that seemed essential to the discharge of his task: the Labour councillor has sometimes been torn between loyalty to the 'larger good' thus represented (and as accepted and enforced in the Corporation by his Party), and the human needs and complaints of his constituents, who are required to accept the conditions thus provided for them. The councillor, like the social worker, the teacher, the housing manager, the police and others, has had to struggle against fatigue and cynicism, continuously trying to renew his idealism.

What of the Labour councillor's ideology and the effects it had upon his civic rôle? There has been no comprehensive study of the way in which social democracy was conceived in Glasgow, and the way in which it has operated. Did Labour councillors think in terms of the scope for 'socialism in one city', or were they pragmatists? It would seem that most of them had a sense of their rôle as propagandists within the general Labour movement, as critics of the capitalist system, as amenders of it, if not outright enemies. But the Holy Grail of a new society receded, once within the City Chambers. For there the immensely complicated agenda of planning and administrative problems, and the almost day-to-day emergency needs of the city predominated: politics took on a managerial rather than an ideological content: the mission to pull down capitalism sank into abeyance. But the other kind of idealism could still operate – trying to make life more bearable for some, moving toward a better society in which people might live a freer life, reducing the great wastage of social and individual talent that was so obvious in the city. As one Labour councillor put it, poets and some politicians are both dreamers of dreams, and both have difficulties in communicating their dreams to the masses.

So it was that the emphasis was placed on welfare, amelioration and improvement, centred especially upon the housing and spatial planning programme. Though this has created problems of heavy subsidy and high rates, the city and its region have acquired more state-assisted houses, Comprehensive Development Area facilities and motorways than most areas in Britain. The social capital and the infrastructure, to use two favourite planning terms, have been largely remade, and at great cost. Glasgow, partly for reasons of its own past, underwent a redevelopment 'storm'.

Meanwhile the Labour Council inherited from the bourgeoisie the problem of maintaining social coherence and minimising anti-social behaviour. These the Council have dealt with, working largely through the Corporation's control of a high proportion of the city's housing stock. They have tried to operate upon deprivation in order to arrest disintegration of the family and the neighbourhood, and have used the welfare services to relieve the worst casualties.

The two major parties in the Corporation, Labour and Progressive (Conservative), shared the general belief that housing had priority. The differences lay in the view taken of private housing and the level of rents: the Conservatives would have made more land available for private enterprise housing, and would have charged higher rents, closer to the economic cost of housing provision. Labour policy has resulted in a lack of private house ownership which has deprived Glasgow people of the greatest of anti-inflationary nest-eggs. It may also have done much damage to labour mobility so that, as Professor MacKay of Aberdeen has remarked, it 'may come a close second to the Berlin Wall as the most formidable obstacle to geographical mobility yet devised by man'.

There is a further element to be considered: it is the middle class from which came the philanthropy and voluntarism of the past. A kind of surveillance of city life, acting as a check upon local government and initiating projects where there have been gaps, was active in the city from the nineteenth century and well into the twentieth, based upon a continuity of managerial and professional classes with a civic and communal sense. But there has been a serious loss of such bourgeois presence and participation in Glasgow. This has been partly because the middle class have abdicated, moving from the city, and partly because they have been to a large degree effectively excluded from local and political life. Bureaucracy, by its nature, cannot respond to all needs, even pressing ones, such as child deprivation, battered wives and inept housing provision, and so is in need of the the the voluntarist watchdog.

Certainly a good deal of civic interest remains, as in so many charitable organisations still continuing, and in the New Glasgow Society, the Civic Trust and the West End Preservation Society. But the need to keep alive the voluntarist principle, with its powers of scrutiny, criticism and initiative, is probably greater than ever in Glasgow. This is, however, to suggest a middle-class monitoring of Labour civic policy, a notion unacceptable to many. Some argue that the real solution lies in making real participatory communities of working class neighbourhoods, so that the correction of bureaucratic policies may come from those affected. Perhaps a combination of such neighbourhood participation and generalised voluntarism is necessary where municipal collectivism is far advanced as in Glasgow.

There appears to have been little misgiving among Labour councillors that the Corporation was acquiring too high a proportion of the housing stock, necessarily imposing on the city the duty of its allocation and administration. On the contrary, the Corporation seems to have believed that the only way to plan and to administer the city was by this very device of owning a high proportion of its social capital. Moreover publicly-owned housing is one of the most powerful of tools for the redistribution of incomes toward the poorer end of the scale. But the impairment of the privately rented sector and the decimation of owner-occupancy has opened up the prospect of a city almost entirely of public tenants. The Housing Corporation, founded in 1964, is an autonomous agency intended to arrest the decay of the private rental sector, as well as to assist in the rehabilitation of older privately-rented property, an operation which the Corporation has tended to regard as too complicated. The Housing Corporation also has a responsibility for those groups not typically catered for by municipal housing policy – the old, single people, students. The Housing Corporation was imposed from outside Glasgow: it was a response to a set of priorities that had been established in the general political context of Britain, made operative in Glasgow and the West of Scotland as part of a national programme.

The economic content of Labour's policy in Glasgow has been largely based on the hope that the improved infrastructure (the road system, Central Redevelopment Areas, Abbotsinch Airport etc.), together with the taking up by firms of the government's regional incentives, would create conditions that would cause the local economy to attract the necessary new industry upon which diversification and recovery could be based. The infrastructure approach has the advantage of avoiding the problem of making invidious decisions at the level of firms: by providing facilities available to all, rather than helping some firms and not others, such a policy appealed to both Labour and Conservative Parties. Unfortunately, however, it largely failed to bring the desired results in Glasgow.

The bitter lesson seems to be that the economy behaves largely according

to its own rules: innovative and efficient management and a productive
labour force have not been induced to any serious extent by infrastructure
and regional incentives.

The dramatic progress in the early and mid-'seventies of the Scottish
National Party may bring profound changes in urban politics and government in the West of Scotland. But the historically generated pattern with
its many problems will still be there. They will be inherited by any
devolved or independent Scottish Parliament.

VII. *The Challenge of Constructive Contraction*

THE TWO major syndromes of Glasgow's experience over the past century have been considered: the growth on so great a scale before 1914, and the decline within the generation since 1945. A third phase overlaps the second, that of controlled contraction.

The state, since 1945, has accepted a range of responsibilities unthinkable in the nineteenth century, and, indeed, as late as the 1920s. They include full employment, the welfare state, regional development, the taking into the public sector of whole ranges of industry and the provision of the conditions of survival in much of the private sector. But it is only in the last two decades or so that a yet further challenge has presented itself: how to conduct a massive contraction in the case of a civic and regional economy such as that of Glasgow, and at the same time renew and reinvigorate it. The region's economy is thus part of a national problem involving decisions about the shape and proportions of the mixed economy taken over-all, and as it will manifest itself on a regional basis.

In many respects the experience of Glasgow since 1945, in spite of its intensity, is a general one. It is now apparent that the large cities of the past, especially in North-Western Europe and America, are undergoing changes that it is impossible to resist. People and jobs are increasingly abandoning the centres of such cities, moving outward to form suburbs and even new centres. Since 1961 the area governed by the Greater London Council has lost nearly a million people and half a million manufacturing jobs. The same trend is apparent in Liverpool, Manchester and Birmingham. But Glasgow is perhaps the most dramatic case among the British provincial cities. It is as though the economy and society, by a kind of consensus, wished to abandon, as places of work and living, its older focal urban centres, with their intimacy and congestion, and substitute something different – a kind of writing off of the past and an entering upon the new.

But an operation of contraction, especially under public aegis, is so much more difficult than one of expansion. It is likely, as in Glasgow, to consist

H

of a negative selection process, so that the recipients of higher incomes, the possessors of greater skills, the more socially aware, remove themselves and their families. Businesses undergo the same kind of self-selection: those with the initiative and resources to make a new beginning on a new site will do so: those without will remain in the old setting. With these trends a city may become a kind of residue, in which are consolidated and confirmed social problems that involve rising social costs and declining morale.

Much depends upon the context within which contraction takes place. If this fundamental change occurs when the region in which the city is located is prosperous, capable of attracting investment (the most common situation), then the changes necessary in the city are much eased. But where the region too is contracting or stagnating the process is much more difficult. The same argument applies on the national scale: while the economy as a whole is generating fairly high employment, output and population growth, it is easier to handle the contraction of a city without acute political tensions – elements of growth can be redeployed without too much difficulty. Where these conditions do not apply, the shifts between and within regions necessary for constructive contraction can be much more difficult. The future of Glasgow must therefore be seen in terms of the problems confronting the Strathclyde Region and the national economy. There is here a good deal of scope for conflict between District, Regional and National governments, centring upon their respective powers, particularly over expenditure.

If the challenge is to be met positively, so that Glasgow may assume a new form and a new identity, it is necessary for the various levels of government concerned to arrive at a more or less agreed conception of how Glasgow City District and Strathclyde Region should look over the next generation and beyond. The critical problem will be the relationship to be aimed at between jobs and social capital, especially housing.

The job level will be partly a question of the city's attractiveness to industry (itself much affected by government incentives) and partly a question of the kind of reputation the city has for labour relations, efficiency and amenity. It will also depend upon how far the government will act directly, locating within the city elements of the national bureaucracy and of the public sector of industry. If industry, public or private, is brought to Glasgow, or maintained there by subsidy in order to create employment irrespective of costs, then the productivity of the nation as a whole (whether thought of as Scotland or the United Kingdom) will, of course, diminish: there is therefore a severe limit to this kind of policy.

There are no signs of the trade unions being prepared to accept a wage level lower for the region than for elsewhere. This was one of the mechanisms of nineteenth-century Britain that attracted work to the workers, but would appear now to be unacceptable.

There is the further circumstance that advanced economies show signs of continuously shrinking their manufacturing sectors and expanding the service element. It may be that the future of a city like Glasgow will lie more in providing commercial premises and service jobs of one kind or another rather than industrial ones. Here is yet a further long-term factor of which account must be taken: there may be some danger of thinking in terms of yesterday's problem of employment.

But one of yesterday's problems will remain, that of housing. The City District has an enormous stake in making municipal housing work, for it has taken the most important single element of the social life of Glasgow into its own hands.

For good or ill, the City District and the Region are dependent upon public manipulation by politicians and bureaucrats of the economy and society, both at the national and regional levels, on such a scale and of such a degree of complexity that the framework of analysis is critical. Whereas the businessmen of Glasgow's Victorian heyday could take as given the major parameters within which they operated their enterprises, relying on the market mechanism to determine them, these parameters themselves have now been largely taken within public control and hence are matters for public discussion and interlocking decision. These are the conditions upon which the new Scottish Development Agency has entered upon its task.

To the job level it will be necessary to adjust the housing and general social capital programme. Just as the city must be designed as an economic entity, so too its provision of social facilities must also be the outcome of conscious decision: this must be in terms of amount, form and spatial distribution.

Glasgow must thus be, to a considerable degree, for a time at least, taken into wardship, a deficit city to an extent greater than most, drawing upon the general resources of the nation and perhaps the EEC, and subject to a high degree of regional and national control.

But it is essential that contraction, if it is to be constructive, should involve the sense of identity of Glaswegians and inspire their initiatives. A city must draw upon the interests and energies of its people if it is truly to flourish. It will not be easy to combine such commitment and involvement with the extent and intricacy of the decisions that will be necessary to engender the necessary renewal on the diminished scale.

Postscript

IT WAS announced in May 1976 that a plan had been formulated to invest £120 m. in the rehabilitation of Glasgow's East End, as extended by the creation of the City District, affecting some 70,000 people in some 3,500 acres. The money will be spent over the eight years to 1984, in the worst remaining areas of urban deprivation, from Glasgow Green in the centre of the city, eastward to Shettleston, and southward to include Bridgeton and Cambuslang. An additional recovery programme of £20 m. for Cambuslang has already been embarked upon. New building, combined with modernisation of older houses, will be undertaken, together with industrial and commercial development, recreational areas and new roads. Houses will be provided both for rent and for sale.

The programme, in addition to being of great importance in itself, is an experiment in co-operation between authorities and agencies. There will be a governing committee of the Scottish Office chaired by an Under Secretary of State. The Scottish Development Agency will have general responsibility, with the City District and Strathclyde Region also involved. The housing will be built by the Scottish Special Housing Association. Much of the planning staff will be those at East Kilbride, formerly intended to design Stonehouse New Town.

The plan is a conscious decision by the Scottish Office, with the support of the City District and the Region (indeed under pressure from them) to abandon the New Town notion in the form of Stonehouse, and to use the resources thus represented for the rehabilitation of the eastern parts of Glasgow. It is also an experiment in planning in a co-ordinated way a large part of a great city. It will use not, as in the past, the city's ideas alone, subject to Scottish Office approval, but will operate in a co-ordinated way, under a public authority, in the form of the Scottish Development Agency. It will be, in short, both an effort in reconstruction and an experiment in government. As such it will be unique in Britain. Its progress will be watched with great interest.

A second new beginning has been announced since the life of the Corporation ended. It is much smaller, but has its own importance. Glasgow

District Council and Strathclyde Region propose to spend some £12 m. to modernise the 900 or so houses of Blackhill and to create in the neighbour-hood a new level of amenity. Instead of writing the area off and clearing the site, the Council will attempt a costly experiment in rehabilitation. It is important that careful thought be given to the programme so that it may succeed, and so that the experience gained can be monitored and made generally available.

Bibliography

A list of works concerned with Glasgow over the past century

I   *Glasgow and its Region, 1875–1975*

Cairncross, A. K., *The Scottish Economy* (1954).
Cunnison, J. and Gilfillan, J. B. S., *Glasgow* (Third Statistical Account of Scotland) (1958).
Glasgow Herald Annual Trades Review.
McDougall, Ian, ed., *An Interim Bibliography of the Scottish Working Class Movement* (Scottish Committee, Society for the Study of Labour History) (Edinburgh, 1965).
MacLaren, A. Allan, *Social Class in Scotland: Past and Present* (Edinburgh, 1976).
Miller, R. and Tivy, J., *The Glasgow Region* (Glasgow, 1958).
Moss, Michael S., and Hume, John R., *Engineering and Shipbuilding in the West of Scotland* (1976).
Oakley, C. A., *The Second City* (1946).
Slaven, Anthony, *The Development of the West of Scotland* (1975).
Smith, Roger, 'Multi-Dwelling Building in Scotland 1780–1970 with special reference to the Clyde Valley', in Sutcliffe, A. ed., *Multistorey Living: the working-class experience* (1974).

II   *Glasgow, 1875–1945*

Anon., *Minutes of Evidence taken before Glasgow Municipal Commission on the Housing of the Poor* (1904).
– *Royal Commission on the Poor Laws, Report on Scotland* (1909).
– *Commission of Inquiry into Industrial Unrest: No. 8 Division: Scotland* (Cd. 8669, 1917).
– *Royal Commission on the Housing of the Industrial Population of Scotland* (Cd. 8731, 1917).
– *The Scottish Socialists. A Gallery of Contemporary Portraits* (1931).
Allan, C. M., 'The Genesis of British Urban Redevelopment, with special reference to Glasgow', *Economic History Review* (1965).
Best, Geoffrey, 'The Scottish Victorian City', *Victorian Studies* (1967–8).
Brogan, Colm, *The Glasgow Story* (1952).

Brown, D. Walker, *Clydeside Litterateurs* (1897).

Bull, H. W., *Working Class Housing in Glasgow 1866–1902* (Strathclyde University M.Litt. thesis) (1974).

Butt, John, *The Industrial Archaeology of Scotland* (1967).

– 'Working Class Housing in Glasgow 1851–1914', in Chapman, S. D., ed., *The History of Working Class Housing* (1971).

Buxton, N. K., 'The Scottish Shipbuilding Industry between the Wars', *Business History* (1968).

Byres, T. J., *The Scottish Economy During the Great Depression 1873–1896* (Glasgow University B.Litt. thesis) (1963).

– 'Entrepreneurship in the Scottish Heavy Industries, 1870–1900', in Payne, P. L., *Studies in Scottish Business History* (1967).

Cairncross, A. K., *Home and Foreign Investment 1870–1913* (1953).

Chalmers, A. K., *Public Health Administration in Glasgow: the writings of James Burn Russell* (1905).

– *The Health of Glasgow, 1818–1925* (1930).

Checkland, S. G., 'The British Industrial City as History: the Glasgow Case', *Urban Studies* (1964).

– *Scottish Banking, a history 1695–1973* (1975).

Cooper, S., *John Wheatley: a study in labour history* (University of Glasgow Ph.D. thesis) (1974).

Cowan, Evelyn, *Spring Remembered, a Scottish Jewish Childhood* (1974).

Dugdale, James and Crathorne, Nancy, *Tennants' Stalk: the story of the Tennants of the Glen* (1973).

Ferguson, T., *Scottish Social Welfare, 1864–1914* (1958).

Fisher, Peter H., *Housing in Glasgow, 1919–1939* (University of Glasgow thesis, Diploma in Town and Regional Planning) (1968).

Gallacher, William, *Revolt on the Clyde* (1936).

Glasier, J. B., *On Strikes* (n.d., 1890?).

Gomme, Andor and Walker, David, *Architecture of Glasgow* (1968).

Hanley, Clifford, *Dancing in the Streets* (1958).

Hume, John, *The Industrial Archaeology of Glasgow* (1975).

– J. and Moss, M., *Clyde Shipbuilding from Old Photographs* (1975).

Hutchison, Ian G., *Politics and Society in Mid-Victorian Glasgow 1846–1886* (Edinburgh University Ph.D. thesis) (1974).

Kellas, J., 'Highland migration to Glasgow and the origin of the Scottish Labour Movement', *Bulletin of the Society for the Study of Labour History* (1966).

Kellett, John R., *Glasgow, a Concise History* (n.d.).

– *The Impact of Railways on Victorian Cities* (1969).

Kendal, Walter, *The Revolutionary Movements in Britain, 1900–21* (1969).

Laidlaw, S., *Glasgow Common Lodging Houses and the People living in them* (1956).

Lythe, S. G. E. and Butt, J., *An Economic History of Scotland, 1100–1939* (1975).

MacLean, Iain S., *The Labour Movement in Clydeside, 1914–21* (University of Oxford Ph.D. thesis) (1970).

McArthur, A. and Long, K., *No Mean City*, first published 1935 (new edition 1964).

McCaffrey, John, 'The Irish Vote in Glasgow in the Later Nineteenth Century', *Innes Review* (1970).

– *Political Reactions in the Glasgow Constituencies at the General Elections of 1885 and 1886* (Glasgow University Ph.D. thesis) (1971).

– 'Origins of Liberal Unionism in the West of Scotland', *Scottish Historical Review* (1971).

McCrone, Guy, *Wax Fruit* (1948).

Middlemass, R. K., *The Clydesiders: a left-wing struggle for parliamentary power* (1965).

Milton, Nan, *John MacLean* (1973).

Morton, G. M., *The Layout of Glasgow Corporation Housing Schemes, 1919–39* (University of Glasgow thesis, Diploma in Town and Regional Planning) (1968).

Moss, Michael and Hume, J., *Glasgow in Old Photographs*, Vols. I and II (1975).

Muir, J. H., *Glasgow in 1901* (Glasgow, 1901).

Ochojna, A. D., *Lines of Class Distinction: the Economic and Social History of the British Tramcar with special reference to Edinburgh and Glasgow* (University of Edinburgh Ph.D. thesis) (1975).

Payne, Peter L., ed., *Studies in Scottish Business History* (1967).

Reid, Fred, Review of Thompson (1971) in *Bulletin of the Society for the Study of Labour History* (1972).

Robertson, A. J., 'The decline of the Scottish Cotton Industry, 1860–1914', *Business History* (1970).

Roxburgh, James M., *The School Board of Glasgow 1873–1919* (1971).

Russell, J. B., 'Life in One Room' (1888), in Chalmers (1905).

Scott, W. R. and Cunnison, J., *The Industries of the Clyde Valley during the War* (Oxford, 1927).

Sillitoe, P. J., *Cloak without Dagger* (1955).

Simpson, Michael, *Middle Class Housing and the Growth of Suburban Communities in the West End of Glasgow, 1830–1914* (Glasgow University M.Litt. thesis) (1970).

– 'Urban Transport and the Development of Glasgow's West End', *Journal of Transport History* (1972).

Slaven, Anthony, 'The Dixon Enterprises' in Payne ed. (1969).

– 'A Shipyard in Depression: John Brown's of Clydebank' (University of Glasgow Discussion Paper) (1976).

Tarn, J. N., 'Housing in Liverpool and Glasgow, the growth of civic responsibility', *Town Planning Review* (1969).

Thompson, L., *The Enthusiasts. A Biography of John and Katherine Bruce Glasier* (1971).
Weir, Molly, *Shoes were for Sunday* (1970).

III   *Glasgow 1945–75*

Anon (in series) *Annual Reports of Glasgow's various Departments: Education, Social Work, Police, Fire.*
– *The First Glasgow Development Plan* (The Bruce Plan) Corporation of Glasgow (1945).
– *The Clyde Valley Plan* (1946).
– *Central Scotland: a programme of growth and development* (Toothill Plan) (1963).
– *Royal Commission on Local Government in Scotland* (Wheatley Report) (1966–9).
– *Glasgow Central Area* (Corporation of Glasgow Planning Department) (1975).
– *Oceanspan Report*, Scottish Council (Development and Industry) (1970).
– *West Central Scotland Plan* (1974).
– *Census Indicators of Deprivation. Working Note No. 6. Great Britain* (ECUR Division, Department of the Environment) (1975).
– *Three Glasgow Writers* (1976).
Abercrombie, Sir Patrick and Matthew, Robert H., *The Clyde Valley Regional Plan*, (1949).
Alexander, K. J. W., 'A work-in reassessed', *New Society*, 20 September (1973).
– and Jenkins, C. L., *Fairfields, a study of industrial change* (1970).
Boden, Sheena A., *Green Belt Policy . . . with reference to the West Midlands and the Clyde Valley* (University of Glasgow, Diploma in Town and Regional Planning thesis) (1969).
Brand, Jack, *et al.*, *Political Stratification and Democracy* (1970).
Brennan, T., *Reshaping a City* (1959).
Brown, Gordon, ed., *The Red Paper on Scotland* (Edinburgh, 1975).
Cable, J. V., 'Glasgow's motorways: a technological blight', *New Society*, 5 September (1975).
– 'Glasgow: Area of Need', in Brown (1975).
Cameron, G. C., 'Economic Analysis for a declining urban economy', *Scottish Journal of Political Economy* (1971).
– and Johnson, K. N., 'Comprehensive Urban Renewal and Industrial Relocation – the Glasgow Case', in Cullingworth, J. B. and Orr, S., eds., *Urban and Regional Studies, a Social Science Approach* (1969).
Campbell, Duncan, ed., *Billy Connolly. The authorised version* (1976).
Carter, C. J., *Comparative Studies in the Post-war Industrial Geography of the Clydeside and West Midland Conurbations* (University of Glasgow Ph.D. thesis) (1972).

Craig, David, 'The Radical Literary Tradition', in Brown (1975).

Cramond, R. D., *Housing Policy in Scotland 1919–1964* (University of Glasgow Research Papers) (1966).

– *Allocation of Council Houses* (University of Glasgow Occasional Paper No. 1) (1964).

Cullingworth, J. B., *A Profile of Glasgow Housing* (University of Glasgow Occasional Paper No. 8) (1965).

– and Watson, D. J., *Housing in Clydeside 1970* (1971).

Damer, Sean, 'Wine Alley: the Sociology of a Dreadful Enclosure', *Sociological Review*, Vol. 22 No. 2 (1974).

– *Working Class Housing and Working Class Incorporation: Glasgow 1861–1919* (University of Glasgow Discussion Paper in Sociological Research) (1976).

– and Madigan, Ruth, 'The Housing Investigator', *New Society*, July (1974).

Davidson, R. N., *Aspects of the Distribution of Employment in Glasgow* (University of Glasgow Ph.D. thesis) (1968).

Edwards, M. K., *The Provision of Community Facilities in Drumchapel* (University of Glasgow thesis, Diploma in Town and Regional Planning) (1970).

Engelman, Stephen R., *The Employment Effects of Housing Relocation* (Research Paper, Department of Social and Economic Research, University of Glasgow) (1975).

Farmer, Elspeth and Smith, Roger, 'Overspill Theory: a Metropolitan Case Study' (Glasgow), *Urban Studies* (1975).

Ferguson, Thomas and Cunnison, James, *In Their Early Twenties: A Study of Glasgow Youth* (Oxford, 1956).

Firn, John, 'External Control and Regional Policy', in Brown (1975).

Forbes, J. and MacBain, J. (eds.), *The Springburn Study* (Glasgow, 1967).

Forsyth, David J. C., *U.S. Investment on Scotland* (1971).

Granick, David, *The European Executive* (1962).

Grieve, R. and Robertson, D. J., *The City and the Region* (University of Glasgow Occasional Paper No. 2) (1964).

Hammond, G. D., *A Controversial Airport* (University of Glasgow B.Phil. thesis) (1969).

Hart, T., *The Comprehensive Development Area* (University of Glasgow Occasional Paper No. 9) (1967).

Hay, D. Roy and McLaughlan, J., 'The UCS Work-in: an interim catalogue', *Scottish Labour History Bulletin*, No. 8 (1974).

– 'The Oral History of Upper Clyde Shipbuilders: a Preliminary Report', *Oral History* (1974).

Henderson, R. A., 'Industrial Overspill from Glasgow', *Urban Studies* (1974).

Herron, Frank, 'Redundancy and Redeployment from UCS, 1969–71', *Scottish Journal of Political Economy* (1972).

House, Jack, *Glasgow Old and and New* (1974).

Jackson, Peter, *Local Authority Public Expenditure: a case study of Glasgow 1948/1970* (University of Stirling Ph.D. thesis) (1975).

Jacobs, Sidney, *The Right to a Decent House* (1976).

Jephcott, Pearl, *Time of One's Own* (1967).

– *Homes in High Flats* (1971).

Johnston, T. L., Buxton, N. K. and Mair, D., *Structure and Growth of the Scottish Economy* (1971).

Jury, A. G., *Housing Centenary, a Review of Municipal Housing in Glasgow from 1866–1966* (Glasgow Corporation Housing Committee) (1966).

Kearsley, G. W. and Srivastava, S. R. 'The Spatial Evolution of Glasgow's Asian Community', *Scottish Geographical Magazine* (September, 1974).

Kellas, J., *The Scottish Political System* (new ed., 1975).

Leonard, Tom, *Poems* (Dublin, 1973).

Liverani, Mary Rose, *The Winter Sparrows, a Glasgow Childhood* (1976).

Lochhead, Liz, *Memo for Spring* (Edinburgh, 1972).

Lowe, James, *British Steam Locomotive Builder* (1975).

Mack, John A., 'Full Time Miscreants, Delinquent Neighbourhoods and Criminal Networks', *British Journal of Sociology* (March, 1964).

Mansley, R. D., *Areas of Need in Glasgow*, Corporation of Glasgow Planning Department (1972).

McCrone, G., *Scotland's Economic Progress 1951–1960: A Study in Regional Accounting* (1965).

Morgan, Edwin, *Glasgow Sonnets* (1972).

Morton, G. M., *The Layout of Glasgow Corporation Housing Schemes* (1968).

Mulrine, Stephen, *Poems* (1971).

Murnaghan, P. E., *Glasgow's CDAs* (University of Glasgow thesis, Diploma in Town and Regional Planning) (1974).

Noble, Graham, 'In Defence of Easterhouse', *New Society*, 20 August (1970).

Norman, P., 'The Impact of local authority decisions on local communities in Glasgow', in Brand, J. and Cox, M., eds., *The Urban Crisis* (1975).

Orr, S. C., 'Urban Renewal in Glasgow', *Scottish Journal of Political Economy* (1959).

Patrick, James, *A Glasgow Gang Observed* (1973).

Reid, James, *Alienation* (1972).

Reid, J. M., *James Lithgow, Master of Work* (1964).

Robertson, D. J. and Grieve, Sir Robert, *The City and Region* (University of Glasgow Occasional Paper No. 2) (1964).

Scott, Wilson, Kirkpatrick and Partners, *Greater Glasgow Transportation Study*, Vols 1–5 (Corporation of Glasgow) (1964–74).

Smith, Roger 'The Origins of Scottish New Towns Policy and the Founding of East Kilbride', *Public Administration* (1974).

Srivastava, Sheila, *The Asian Community in Glasgow* (University of Glasgow Ph.D. thesis) (1976).

Thomas, John, *The Springburn Story. The History of the Scottish Railway Metropolis* (1964).

Welch, Richard V., 'Immigrant Manufacturing Industry established in Scotland between 1945 and 1968', *Scottish Geographical Magazine* (1970).

Wilson, J. G., *The Trial of Peter Manuel* (1959).

Index

Figures in **bold type** indicate whole chapters or sections. Alphabetical order: word-by-word, to first comma or colon. 'G' means Glasgow.

and a green belt, 66; Barlow Report (1940), 66; and a 'new town' (East Kilbride), 67, 71; new housing estates (peripheral), 67–8; and need for 'amenities', for community life, 68–9; abolition of restriction on public houses, 69; 'overspill', 69–70, 71–3 *passim*; slum clearance, 70, 72; battle of densities, *q.v.*, 70–1; another 'new town' (Cumbernauld), 71; 'Cumbernauld conditions', 71; general 'overspill' policy (dispersal) adopted, 71–3 *passim*; re-location of industry, a government responsibility, 71, 72; G Corporation, and other local authorities, agree on 'overspill' policy, 71; policy from 1960 on, 72–3; state of housing stock (c. 1960), 72; fall of population (1961–75), 72; new industries do not come as hoped for, 72; Housing Corporation and Planning Exchange, 73; cost of regeneration *not* ascertainable, 92

civic authority and government of G (*see also* Corporation of G *and* Labour Town Council), 14, 28–30; perceptive men in, 11; party politics in (1933), 37–8

Civic Trust, 94

class consciousness, and differentiation of classes, 2, 22–4, 32, 81–3; within the working class, 82

Clyde, River (and estuary), 4, 5; shipbuilding, 3, 5–7 (*see also* Upper Clyde); firms on bank of, 6; new bridges over, 63

Clyde: Tunnel, 75; Valley, 17, 66, 74; Valley Plan, 66, 71, 75

Clyde Shipbuilders and Engineers

Association (employers), 16

Clyde Workers' Committee, 35

Clydebank: sewing-machine factory, 12; coat-of-arms, 12; and Jimmy Reid, 85

Clydeside: complex, 11, 12; concentration of industry and control on (by 1968), 54; construction, examples of, 9; deprivation on, 87; engineering ability, 3; engines, 9; Expressway, 75, 79; foreign owned and controlled industries on, 61; investment in, 60–1; *Litterateurs*, 83, 104; MPs, 37; militancy of workers (1914–18), 34; obsolescence, creeping, 47–8; population variants, 8; rescue operations, 42; success, factors contributing to, 14; workers (labour force), strong bargaining position of, 58; Workers' Committee, 35

Coatbridge (Calderbank Iron Works, J. Dunlop & Co.), 4

Collins, Sons & Co., William (publishers), 55

Colossus, HMS, 9, 10

Colvilles Ltd. (*formerly* David Colville & Sons Ltd., to 1931): rescued by the Lithgows, 42; nationalised (1950), 43; steel reduction plant at Gartcosh, 52–3

Comet, Henry Bell's early steamship, 9; centenary (1912), 9

Communism, and Communist Party on Clydeside (1970), 51, 59, 61, 84

community life, 18–19, 76, 78, 79; provision for, essential in 'new towns' and housing estates, 67–8; self-adjusting and advising municipality, 95; *see also* G 'crosses' *and* 'villages', high-rise flats *and* tenement

I